If all the ladies should know
about spectroscopes and cathode rays,
who will attend to the buttons and breakfasts?

Asked of Wellesly astronomy professor Sarah Whiting by a male colleague in the 1880s.

Wits WonderWoman Project

# THE WITS WONDERWOMAN BOOK
# BUTTONS AND BREAKFASTS

Edited by Margaret Orr, Mary Rorich and Finuala Dowling
Designed by Hybrid

WITS UNIVERSITY PRESS

# CONTENTS

# DEDICATION

This book is dedicated to the X chromosome.

# ACKNOWLEDGEMENTS

Perhaps it takes a village to write a book like this. The writers would like to acknowledge, with gratitude and appreciation, the following villagers:

Our families, significant others, students and colleagues who endured our absences on Writing Retreats and our mental distraction; who offered encouragement and support; and who provided us with provocative and painful experiences to write about.

Our many readers and critics of work-in-progress.

Our donors – Atlantic Philanthropies – who have generously, and trustingly, funded the WonderWoman, GlassBusters, and Frontiers programmes, and some of the costs of this book.

Our portrait photographer, Debbie Yazbek, who did not manage to persuade us to do 'Calendar Girls', but made us feel beautiful nevertheless.

Our designer and illustrator – Karen Lilje – who caught fire and interpreted our ideas and dreams.

Wits, for giving us the edge.

# PREFACE

## This book was born in the steam room of a conference venue behind the boerewors curtain.

It was a venue we[1] used to take women away on extended writing and training retreats, as part of the year-long annual WonderWoman programme (described in more detail at the end of this collection). By far the most interesting part of the retreats were the stories of the women and of Wits that were recounted in the jacuzzi, the change rooms, the cigar lounge, over tea and coffee and whisky and wine, high on the indulgent smell of aromatherapy oils. By 2004, we had taken four groups of women through the programme, and the pressure of the unwritten narratives became irresistible. And so we embarked on a further arduous round of retreats with a self-selected sample group of WonderWomen alumnae who committed themselves to putting together a collection of their reflections on scholarly life, on being a woman and an academic, and on the ineffably interesting environment that is Wits.

Three years later, what has emerged is a 'struggle' document. This is a book about the struggle of a young girl to become a professor; the struggle of women academics to play the WonderWoman game; the struggle to balance a life of possibilities with hard choices and frenetic multi-tasking; the struggle to keep a sense of meaning and direction and – critically – a sense of humour in the journey to and into and through academe. Meta-reflectively, this book has been a struggle to write in ways that offer resonance and fresh meaning to other academic women who have travelled this path with us, wisdom and light to young women coming after us, and some insight to our male counterparts who may be curious as to what it is their female colleagues are really thinking.

Organizational culture is described as the stories an institution tells its members about who we are and how we do things. It is the stories that neophytes are told in order properly to induct them into the culture. This book captures an alternative set of stories – the stories of a university that are not always heard. It is about the twists and turns and detours in the fractal-patterned academic life of women. There are journeys here from dusty township to dental school, from dropout to doctorate. There are testimonies here of careers kept aloft through sexual harassment cases, through pregnancies, cancer, marital breakup and personal despair. In these pages the secret lives of women academics come to

---

1. The authorial 'we' in this sentence refers to myself, Professor Margaret Orr, as director of the Centre for Learning, Teaching & Development; Dr Wendy Orr, director of Transformation and Employment Equity; and Dr Pamela Nichols, director of the Writing Centre, all at the University of the Witwatersrand, Johannesburg, South Africa (colloquially known as 'Wits'). And also, indirectly, to our donors – Atlantic Philanthropies – who had faith in untested ideas and lateral approaches to equity development and transformation, and who have generously – and trustingly – funded a range of our initiatives and programmes to empower black and female academic staff, including the WonderWoman Project, and the costs of this book.

An essential aid
to 'WOMAN-POWER'

Fitness and morale are matters of national concern, and anything that helps to maintain them is a munition of war.

The strain of the times, far from lessening the value of foundation garments, makes them more necessary than ever. For whether she rears a family or mans a range-finder, a woman needs the physical support of a good foundation. Muscular areas and heavy flesh *must* be supported, or excessive fatigue will result. Not only is physical energy reduced, but mental strain is increased and *morale* is undoubtedly affected.

Amongst other munitions of war, Berlei are still making foundations. But they are fewer and in a much smaller range of styles. If you do have difficulty in obtaining a particular Berlei, try another in the same figure-type. Above all, be sure to get a correct true-to-type fitting; in other words, be personally fitted by a trained corsetiere.

*Berlei*

TRUE-TO-TYPE
FOUNDATIONS

# There are journeys here from dusty township to dental school, from dropout to doctorate.

light – the sacrifices they've made in their passionate commitment to their chosen discipline and to their students. Sometimes profoundly solitary, sometimes bolstered by the sisterhood, sometimes warrior-like and sometimes weeping, they've crossed borders and boundaries of the academic and personal unknown. From moving tales of grandmothers and mothers to irreverent satires of university life, the pieces in this book offer an explicit counter-narrative.

The subversive nature of the text in your hands means that we[2] have taken transgressive liberties with various genres. We have not written scholarly, well-footnoted[3] research papers, unhappily for our CVs. We have no 'Seven Secrets of Highly Successful Professors', unfortunately for our bank balances. We have combined sentimental memoirs of life in the groves of academe, with mismatched pieces of semi-scholarly writing, and even some poetry, regrettably for our image as suitably serious intellectuals. We have not – even – resisted the temptation to be scurrilous , scandalous[4], surreal and scathing, alas for our future career prospects.

What is the best analogy to describe this book? Is it a quest story, a Bildungsroman, a picaresque, a written divertimento[5], a random context picture grammar[6]? Told by many voices, this is a story of apprenticeship to life and learning and – ultimately – of a forging of identity. The compilation celebrates the diversity of Wits women in the sounds of their voices, the counterpoint of their ideas and interpretations of life as women and as academics at the University of the Witwatersrand.

In this book, each author could work on her pieces independently from the other authors, if she so wished. However, more often than not, her ideas for a new piece or the refinement of an existing piece were sparked by ideas of others, perhaps in formal reading sessions, or in informal conversations, say at dinners, in the spa or on walks. In this way, the book has become much more complex than it could have been in an environment without interaction.

The common thread of the collection is that we are all women and we have all spent parts of our lives at this university. We believe and trust that you will find some resonance in the versions of life and reality we present.

---

2. This 'we' refers to the varied group of writers and artists who have contributed to this volume.

3. This preface probably has more footnotes than the entirety of the rest of the book.

4. Everything in this book is true, and none of it is true. Where possible, names and details have been changed or obscured to prevent undue embarrassment to the writers and to the people they describe. The thoughts and comments and interpretations are those of the individual writers, and should not – under any circumstances – be taken to reflect the official views of Wits staff or students, or the mission, vision and values of this university.

5. Etymology: Italian, literally, diversion, from *divertire* to divert, amuse, from Latin *divertere*

6. Such a grammar generates pictures through successive refinement. It starts with a blank shape, say a square or a triangle, and divides it iteratively into subshapes. Finally, it assigns a colour to every shape and thus creates an image.

MARY RORICH

# DE HOEK COUNTRY HOUSE – TWELVE WOMEN WRITING

MARY RORICH

Silence in the sizzling drone of beetles.
The dying autumn maize crackling;
birds cry out above a stagnant pool;
wings heavy, surging up then sinking;
doves (cinnamon or laughing?)
gurgling in the darker reaches of branches
despite querulous mynahs.
A soundscape in which to paint a red dragonfly
helicopter-like with scarlet velvet cab and fiery proboscis.
*A frame for turning interior thoughts into public words.*


Chandeliers set high against wooden eaves
and sloping ceilings;
brass engaging dappled sunlight,
prints, too, of fish and fowl.
Iced carafes and chewy peppermints
above broad oak-leafed patterns
and places for sixteen;
heavy doors open onto wine for lunch and glasses;
An interior silence of tap-tap-tapping;
*Narratives lonely before they are shared.*

# MRS LIVINGSTONE, I PRESUME?

PROFESSOR LIVINGSTONE

One of the major motivating forces that got me through the tedious haul of completing my doctorate was the joyful anticipation that I could escape the ongoing battle to be called Ms, rather than Miss or Mrs. Back in the heady days of early feminism, insisting on the 'Ms' had seemed like a big deal, a hugely important and wildly exciting transgression and challenge to the hegemony. It became more than a little tedious for many of us, however, insisting on it to colleagues, doctors, repairmen, and your child's teacher, who had never heard the usage, or – if they had – found it silly and irrelevant. It didn't help that my life was in Pretoria at that stage, so I had, more often than not, to use the Afrikaans version ('Me' – pronounced [mə], like a constipated bleat from a sheep with low self esteem).

So, while slogging through pages of footnotes and interminable chapter revisions in my thesis (often with a baby clamped to one breast while I typed with my free hand), I looked forward to the golden day when I could respond to the question 'Is that Miss or Mrs?' with the insouciant answer 'Actually, it's Doctor.'

Alas for my illusions. Society, even in the new millennium, battles to recognize that women have titles. Telephone salesmen and -women, plumbers, and dishwasher repairmen still persist in assuming that the female voice answering the phone or the door must be the lady of the house, and thus has to be Mrs (or maybe Miss, and perhaps – if they're really

Sensitive New Age types – Ms) Livingstone. Dr Livingstone is clearly your husband, and the one they really want to talk to.

It's 6 pm, I've just dragged myself home from work, am busy engaging with a six-year-old who wants a day's worth of attention right now and the phone rings.
'Hello,' I say.
'Is that Mrs Livingstone?' an unbearably bright voice chirps.
'No.'
Silence.
'Ummm... who is it then?'
'Whom did you think you were phoning?'
'Ummm... Dr Livingstone.'
'Therefore I must be...?' and I put the phone down.

At a Game store I give my credit card to the woman at the till. Peering at it, she asks 'Is this your credit card?'
Thinking I might have given her my son's medical aid card or something equally inappropriate I look at it and say 'Yes, it is.'
'But it says Dr Livingstone...' she replies.
'Yes it does?' (This conversation is making no sense to me.)
'But... you're a woman.'
Well, thank you for pointing that out. It certainly is useful information.

And then there was the time I was invited for an interview at UCT[1]. I was put up at the Hilton (UCT clearly wanting to lure senior staff with appropriate status and comfort).

---

1. The University of Cape Town

When I arrived, the receptionist asked, 'And when will Dr Livingstone be arriving, Mrs Livingstone?'

But perhaps that's only the less educated classes, or only in fleeting contacts with people you don't know? Sorry, no. Your tax accountant will look at you in bemusement, and then rather call you by your first name.

we would be able to leave the Miss/Mrs/Ms debate behind us? But we didn't allow for the force of social stereotype which has cast professors as aging white males in baggy tweed, lost in the midst of an interminable bad-hair day.

Asserting professorial title and status leads – more often than not – to nervous titters

## Dr Livingstone is clearly your husband, and the one they really want to talk to.

The entire medical profession thinks that non-medical doctorates are just pretentious 'play-play' titles anyway, so your child's paediatrician and your gynaecologist and their receptionists will opt for a default 'Mrs'. The headmaster at your child's school (already horribly embarrassed by your flagrantly single-parent status) will prefer to call you nothing, and your hairdresser finds the whole concept of a female professor hilarious and calls everyone 'lovey', so that's a lost cause.

Having become disillusioned in the totemic force of The Doctorate, some of us pinned our hopes on the title of professor. Surely, we thought, surely once we had endured the arcane rituals of academic promotion, published the books, acquired the requisite Research Voyager Miles, impressed the selection committee, delivered the inaugural lecture and 'become' a professor... surely then

and bemused incomprehension on the part of functionaries (the official at the driver's licence department, the estate agent, the bank clerk) filling in your details on one of those forms that attempt to capture the complexities of your identity in neat computer-generated boxes and block capitals.

I arrive at an up-market private clinic early one morning, my stomach empty apart from butterflies. My doctor has booked me in for some minor but stressful day surgery. His receptionist had made all the arrangements, confirming with the clinic that Professor Livingstone required day-ward accommodation.

I present myself at the desk. The Matron is furious with me. She has allocated Professor Livingstone to the men's day ward, and is exasperated that I have arrived minus the qualifying genital appendage. There is no

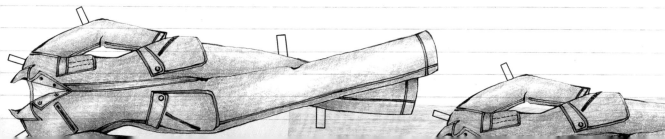

But we didn't allow for the force of
social stereotype which has cast professors as
aging white males in baggy tweed,
lost in the midst of an interminable bad-hair day.

free bed in the women's day ward. I am made to feel as negligent and irresponsible as if I had ignored the strict instructions not to eat or drink after midnight. As punishment, I am given the choice of joining the men (in line with my inappropriate pretensions to being something I'm not) or to take a private ward at a higher cost. I agree to take the private ward. My medical aid is not amused, and docks the excess off my salary.

I think I gave up on it all on the day I applied to join Virgin Active. The agent filled in my membership form online.
'Gender?'
Well, that was easy. She pressed 'F'.

'Title?'
'Professor,' I said.
The dropdown menu didn't offer that option. There was 'Reverend' and 'Doctor', but not professor. Perhaps professors don't 'do' gym? There was 'Ms'. So what was it to be? I briefly toyed with 'Reverend', but sighed and agreed to settle for 'Doctor'.
The agent highlighted the choice, clicked, and then blinked at the Error Message. 'INVALID ENTRY' it said, in loud red letters; 'WOULD YOU LIKE TO GO BACK AND CHANGE THE GENDER?' What the hell. 'OK,' I said. 'Enough already. So I'm male. I'm male and it's **Dr** Livingstone.'

Archaeologists dig bones

MOYRA KEANE

# BECOMING MORE OF A PERSON

MOYRA KEANE

But the question still remains:
'Has the complete object been caught in the net?'
I would say, 'Decidedly not!' (D.T. Suzuki, 1986)

It is customary in African culture not to start talking before introducing yourself[1]. My name is Moyra. I work at a university in Johannesburg and have lived in South Africa all my life. For many years I worked in KwaZulu-Natal with students and teachers, teaching science and, in the holidays, taking students away into the wilderness.

I also spent occasional time at the Buddhist Retreat Centre – right at the research site. (My supervisor at Wits laughed at the 'coincidence' when I announced my research plans!) I am an English speaking (only) city dweller, mother, teacher and from a private school background. I have never carried water on my head, nor been a pupil at a rural school.

I have always been interested in learning – but unsure what that may mean. Does it matter who I am? This is how I realized it does.

## EARLY BEGINNINGS
The square, flat backyard in Kensington was grey and cracked – the sun had never discovered it. A small play space and a nuclear family. My father was a reporter. My mother's mother much later asked me if I had known he was a 'stark-raving communist'. My mother cooked and darned socks, wrote magazine articles and worked as a bookkeeper. Keeping the home finances sometimes brought her to tears.
I heard the word 'Sharpeville' for the first time; and Dad didn't come home. Mum told us to be brave, that we might have to go to England suddenly without them, but this was never mentioned again. Perhaps that was when Dad started drinking... I don't remember. In English culture there are many things you don't talk about.

When I went to Roedean (to escape Christian Nationalist Education), Mum said I shouldn't mention that she worked – not that she was asking me to lie exactly – but just not to mention it. I learnt that a working mother was an embarrassment. There was that, and being an atheist, and wearing homemade clothes rather than shopping in London and Paris: I did not quite belong. Not that I understood what my school friends were all so proud about... but this is later.

The square, flat backyard in Kensington was grey and cracked – the loquat tree had a house in it where grown-ups couldn't go. They were too big but I was too small, so I needed to be lifted up to the first branches. Monkey and Snake and Teddy and Tiger and others in the carry-cot came with me to the wooden platform. Not for me the silly-prissy, dressed-up dolls, all stiff and plastic. One day we came home from Granny's and it was raining.

---

1. I once wanted to invite the Inkosi (Chief) to our science festival in Chibini. We had designed some formal invitations. 'No! You can't just send an invitation – just like that,' the principal, Mr Xulu, remonstrated.

## In English culture there are many things you don't talk about.

I asked Kevin to help me into the tree to fetch the drowning group on the platform.

'No! It's raining, Dummy.' So I asked my mother: 'Really!... you shouldn't have left them in the tree...' I didn't want to ask my father, but that was the last option. 'They are only STUFFED ANIMALS!' I went away crying that they had got turned into stuffed animals. Soon afterwards I gave them away as they were only stuffed animals. I entered the grim lifeless world of adulthood.

### SCHOOL
Kevin got this crisp neat school uniform, grey shorts, and grey long socks and shiny black shoes – a little big 'to grow into'. He grasped my mother's hand tightly as he set off to Class One. I was awed. I was jealous. Why couldn't

cells with a very short expiry date. These lost ones his capital and their guilt: my brother.

### AN EASY BIRTH
So when I bounced into the world two years later (this time a planned arrival) with a smile under blond curls and never cried or got sick and could do everything far too soon, there needed to be some leveling... which was often done with the back of a hairbrush. Kevin soon realized he would be spared the hairbrush-whackings: a great advantage in sibling fights.

At six I desperately wanted to play the violin but Mum said I was precocious enough and already played the piano and recorder. When I asked what 'precocious' was she said (to prove the point) 'Look it up!' and I thought

## I learnt that a working mother was an embarrassment.

I go? I could read already and count and add. I wanted to play the piano too like my mother and brother. Why did I have to wait? Seven years old was an eternity away. Maybe he would have used up all the learning by then and there would be none for me.

### A DIFFICULT BIRTH
Their anxiety started on the day he was born. He needed help even then – refusing to emerge without forceps and strangling his first delayed breath with his own umbilical cord. He didn't want this cut, but they did. He breathed at last and he never forgave them. One breath too late: brand new brain

'tuberculosis... osis... sclerosis' and wondered if I was going to die soon. But the dictionary said: 'early development' and I thought this isn't so terrible and didn't understand.

At seven I composed a song for my brother who had rheumatic fever and was always in bed. I wrote the notes neatly in my special theory book: it was in C major and in 4/4 time which I knew was a bit plonky and the base chords were clunky but it fitted with the words. Mrs Gamber glanced at it when I went for my piano lesson: she looked angry (I was scared of her anyway). I knew it wasn't that good but it was my first composition, so perhaps she could help me. We had a strained lesson till Mum came to fetch me. Whispers in the other room. Some suspicion lingered: I didn't understand why. I didn't try to write music again.

WANDERINGS
Then I was old enough to start wandering. We had moved house to Craighall with huge new trees to climb and close to the Jukskei River. I made daily excursions after school

In Grade One I already had feelings of teenage rebellion, premature boredom, confusion, frustration and the growing resignation that there was no meaning to be found. I winged my way through tests and exams – bunking often. In Standard Six there was refuge in Shakespeare, but I stayed at home on the days we had to read aloud. Afrikaans was evil and to fail was honourable; French could have been fun if we had discussed literature but we didn't.

The science teacher said I had a weak character and should give up science. I didn't think much of her character either but wasn't allowed to say so, so I gave up science instead.

on my bicycle to escape from homework and a bullying brother. Down to the river where cool rocks, crunchy dried leaves and perfect sparkling spider webs stirred slight memories of the lost magic. Then some late afternoons I would sit on the deserted steps of the school, overlooking early evening lights and wonder what was going on for all those people in the tiny distant houses. Did they not wish to escape too? When I first discovered the deserted school grounds, I noticed the sign: 'Trespassers will be prosecuted'. I thought 'electrocuted... prosecuted... executed'. This was a little extreme I thought. But then nothing about the adult world made much sense and they were always overreacting. I felt a twinge of fear at being caught, but not enough to make me leave. I'd tell the police who came to arrest me that I couldn't read the sign; or maybe that I hadn't seen the sign. Was it OK to tell a lie to save yourself from being executed? Would I be hanged or guillotined? I thought: this is a cruel world and full of stupid rules.

The maths teacher proclaimed that I did not exist. The science teacher said I had a weak character and should give up science. I didn't think much of her character either but wasn't allowed to say so – so I gave up science instead. The last years of school continued: a low-grade daily war.

AN UNFORTUNATE AFTERNOON
Fifteen-year-old pretensions of being grown-up: Woodstock, marijuana, afternoon clubs, enough pocket money for bus fare home but if I hitchhiked... a brazen-elated stop first to buy amphetamines. He opened the door of the dirty-messed Hillbrow flat. I wondered about the towel around his waist – it wasn't there long.

I only remember crying and pain and shame and crying and time stopping and thinking of my mother (strangely enough) and she was never to know. He shouted, 'Move, bitch!' and I didn't know what he meant and consciousness blurred as I vomited on the

> *In the mind-blowing freedom of campus*
> *there were swarming crowds, boys,*
> *hundreds of buildings,*
> *boys, piles of huge textbooks.*

pavement later, wondering how the world had changed in one afternoon.

## WITS PART 1

I had concluded that life was meaningless, society corrupt and I had no wish to participate. The passive option was to drift into Wits at seventeen – to do a BA – I supposed: English, French, Art History, Philosophy.

Suddenly there was no uniform, no morning assembly, no prefects: delirious freedom. African-print kaftan and sandals and braided hair. 1971 and Santana, Jimi Hendrix and Ram Das. In the mind-blowing freedom of campus there were swarming crowds, boys, hundreds of buildings, boys, piles of huge textbooks. In the stillness of the William Cullen there were even stepladders to reach the high top shelves. Where to go? This was a whole lot worse than anything so far. In the entire year I spoke to no-one – not a single person.

In the English tutorial I got accused of plagiarism in my Chaucer essay. What were my sources? Pain of being singled out: 'sources'? I hadn't known people wrote books about books! Was there no end to this volume of stuff drowning me? 'No, Ma'am,' – the Roedean training surfacing – 'the ideas were mine'. In front of the whole group there were threats of exclusions for cheating. I felt faint with confusion. (I didn't go back.)

In French I got zero for the first essay. Winging it wasn't going to work here! The lecturer performed theatrically in French in front of about 100 students: 'Zero! Zero! No one has ever got zero! How did you manage it?' (I didn't go back.) Art. Art? I didn't know where the art library was and became more and more shy to ask as the months went by. (Eventually I couldn't go back.) Philosophy (my real interest) – I read all of Plato's dialogues – including the footnotes. The first essay was on Aristotle. (I didn't go back.)

## AND THEN?

Through a caring, encouraging violin teacher, I ventured into teacher's college at 26.

I never imagined I'd voluntarily set foot in school again but maybe I could make things different. I didn't want anyone to have the experiences I had had. When I started Physics 1, I was the only girl in the class. Every morning the lecturer glared at me and said: 'You still here?' To be fair, I did ask some dumb questions: 'What's that little ten for?' (as in $6^{10}$).

There was a shocked silence. But I had been out of school for almost ten years and I hadn't done science at school. I'd also never seen a calculator before... and I felt very old at 26. So I read all the school textbooks on weekends, practising to find the weight of the earth and the acceleration of the lift and the momentum of a trolley. I was determined not to drop out and give the lecturer the satisfaction of knowing that I couldn't make it.

The man I was married to was uneasy as I went into second year. He started to object, so I worked at 4 am... and I made it through till fourth year and then also through a BA part-time, which took about eight years while teaching and mothering and looking after in-laws. When I finished the marriage was finished too – or actually it finished much earlier.

### WITS PART 2
As I walk across campus 30 years on, I am amazed and amused at the irony of my being here. I see the new bright-eyed students, hopeful, elated at arriving, over-dressed, lost, free, already under pressure. I sit on selection and readmission committees and hear the ex-perfect students (now in high places) bemoan the current calibre of students with their poor maths marks and their lack of 'everything'. I feel heartsore for those who didn't make it: I know there are many paths to learning and not all of them are smooth.

### AND NOW?
At last I can write what I like how I like (and I've learnt to acknowledge my sources). Not surprisingly, my PhD is still about my learning – with little thanks as usual to formal academia. I get to talk about Ram Das and Plato and science education and gender and trips into the wilderness and encounters with shy students who bring their music and stories into science. I get to do research in Ixopo.

The word 'Ixopo' derives from the onomatopoeic description of the cow's hoof pulling out of the thick wet fertile mud. In the Ixopo valley I love the space, rolling hills, wild river places, pretty goats, open fires, slow pace and vast open sky. I would not love being cold, hungry, beaten at school and having least say as a girl. I would not enjoy chorus-style classrooms that lead to no jobs. I would like my work (our work) to make a difference to the students here, to help rural culture contribute its knowledge to the wider democratic and academic discourse. I do not know what this may be but it would have to have something to do with education and science. And, of course, I want to learn: What matters here? What other ways are there of understanding the world? What does this teach me about myself?

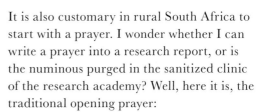

It is also customary in rural South Africa to start with a prayer. I wonder whether I can write a prayer into a research report, or is the numinous purged in the sanitized clinic of the research academy? Well, here it is, the traditional opening prayer:
*May all people in the rural areas, especially in Chibini and Ifafa, have a better future, have enough to eat, gain in confidence, and have meaningful – wonderful – learning experiences so that their knowledge and culture is a resource for all. May I become more of a person here.*

# THE ORANGE NOTEBOOK

TRACY MCLELLAN

At the beginning I had one book with me. It was small, orange, waterproof, with nothing written on its lined pages. I wrote my name and old address on the inside cover, and on the first page a plan of what I wanted to do on a three-month field trip. The first dated entry in my field notebook:

*9 January*
*Locality data from Herbarium sheets, Kew.*
*Inanda, Natal; Bashee River Mouth; Eshowe,*
*Ngotshe Forest; Uvongo side river; Manubi,*
*Transkei; Gwalaweni Forest.*

I came to South Africa in January of 1991, in search of a group of plants, *Begonia dregei*, which grow in the coastal forests on the eastern side of South Africa. I had decided to work on this group a few years previously when my husband took a job at the University of California at Santa Barbara, where there was no job for me. So I gave up doing research on human genetics, and found another project, more in line with what I was really interested in, using these little plants as a 'system' with a great deal of variation in leaf shape that could be studied to understand more general things about how the size and shape of living things can change through evolution. The species group is perfect for this, because the leaves differ between plants, but the plants are so closely related that they can be crossed easily, and therefore the genes that make leaves different shapes ought to be accessible.

When I traced the plants back to their origins, I found that they had been in the collections of botanic gardens in Europe for many years, but their origins before that were unknown. I knew that if my study was to be convincing, I needed plants with known origins in nature. I wrote to anyone I could find an address for in South Africa, had some polite replies, and one collection of seeds from someone whose friend wanted to do a postdoc with my husband. I wrote to the South African expert in the group. She said she was going on one last field trip before she relocated to Edinburgh, and that it would not be to begonia country.

Letters in the 1980s took about six weeks in each direction, and I often forgot what questions I had asked when the replies came. I wrote to someone in the herbarium in Pretoria to ask about locality data, because I wanted to know if the different forms occurred within a small population, or whether they were separate. I got a long explanation of the wonderful system of quarter-degree grid-square mapping, and no answer to my question.

It was becoming obvious that I needed to go to collect the plants myself. At first I was hesitant to be away from my husband for so long. Then I saw a letter to the editor in the journal *Nature* from the Dean of Science at the University of Transkei, asking that people not boycott academics in South Africa, but join him in the struggle to educate blacks. The letter was filled with expressions in Afrikaans and isiXhosa, and barely comprehensible in places; it was the first time I had seen the word Transkei. I looked up Umtata, found that it was not far from Port St Johns, where the highest diversity of *B. dregei* was known, and wrote him a letter, offering my help in education in return for assistance in collecting plants. I got his name wrong, but the letter was answered, and he agreed to provide me with support for my visit. By then my husband had fallen into the grip of a terrible depression, for which he blamed me, and insisted he would get better if I left. The welcome from the University of Transkei had come at an opportune time, when the only way I could deal with my husband was to run away. I raised money, trying normal academic sources that were not interested at least in part because South Africa was not exactly popular in the late 1980s, but succeeding with the American Begonia Society. I moved to North Carolina first, near my parents, and worked there for a few months, before leaving at what should be the right time of year to find the plants with seeds.

him over them. I reassured him, as I had done several years earlier, that I was not in the least interested in doing what he needed to do with the Asian species. He took me to lunch at a pub with a roaring fire, and when we got back to the herbarium, I fell soundly asleep over the dry plants. But I had collected my data, these strange names that sounded like music to me. I got on another overnight plane to Johannesburg, and a short flight to Durban. Five hours to wait for a little bus to Pietermaritzburg, where I attended a botany conference.

Finally, I drove off to Transkei, a 'country' that was not on any map in my atlas published in 1971. I had a ride with Elize, who was hosting me for my visit, and her two daughters. Julia, then aged seven, slept leaned up against her mother as we drove through

## The welcome from the University of Transkei had come at an opportune time, when the only way I could deal with my husband was to run away.

Travelling involved leaving cold, dark, icy North Carolina, taking a plane to even colder New York, another plane to London, where I spent a sleepy day looking at dry plants in the herbarium at Kew, the real beginning of the trip as indicated by my notebook. I had seen only one publication that gave information on the localities where the plants I was studying had been found, but that information was to general region, not specific enough to be able to find them again. The information on the specimens at Kew, as well as what I could learn about varieties of leaf shapes, was essential. My host at Kew had described some species of begonia from Asia, and said that he had another 800 to describe. He was terribly worried that I would compete with

the January greenness of the South coast, past beaches, some patches of indigenous bush but also many areas with nothing but deserts of sugar cane. We took a break at Kokstad, and then the upward climb to Brook's Nek, and the border.

With my first look, I fell in love. The intense green of the steep hills, the winding road down the other side into a different world of small huts and round faces, graceful women in long skirts with heavy loads on their heads. Others might notice the land erosion, that the fields had not been planted this year, perhaps saying, 'These people are so lazy, they are waiting for handouts.' It was a land the way it should be, with trees taller than

Bizarrely,
this place on the other face of the earth,
where people spoke a language
I found totally incomprehensible,
felt like home.

people and rivers with water in them, unlike that unnatural dryness of California. I had fallen in love, but it was not just with the pretty scenery and smiling faces. Bizarrely, this place on the other face of the earth, where people spoke a language I found totally incomprehensible, felt like home.

Thus began several weeks of collecting. We started with the places I had found out about from Kew and the herbarium in Durban, and places that Elize knew. On the first trip we went to Port St Johns, and found plants in two places. In my notebook:

*23 Jan 1991.*
*1) SW facing slope of Mt. Sullivan, and 2) Third Beach, up Gxwaleni River, along banks on rocks. Of the 2 places where begonia was found, leaf shape seemed homogeneous within each.*

the beach, find the river, up the north (shady) side of the river, and then, when the ground gets steep and there are good trees and dense shade, we would find the little plants. The steep areas were often very unstable, and it was difficult to climb around. There are a few plants with horrible stinging hairs, and we learned quickly not to grab them. Sometimes there were only a few begonias, never large or dominant, but we found them in almost every forest patch. We went up and down to the coast, in dust when the sun was out, or in mud when the misty rain fell.

The other plants were infinitely fascinating – the huge flowers, the wide diversity. Birds overhead, the sounds of the loeries and the cicadas in the forests, the cool, moist smell of a forest after walking through a hot sunny grassland. Sometimes, when we were getting

Every day was for work, because it was such a privilege to be able to do science, so interesting, and there is always so much to do. I never understood what it was that other people spent their time doing.

I had an answer for one of my questions about the plants, and spent much of the following ten years documenting their population structure.

I thought we would be able to find plants near waterfalls, as that is where I had found begonias in Trinidad. Elize knew one place that was along the old road to Port St Johns. We walked along the track, and saw some plants up high, then turned a corner, and there was a small waterfall. We had both been right. After locating the places we could from old records, we developed a pattern for looking for more plants – down the road to

to the places where it was dark and moist enough for begonias, it was the smell that indicated this was the right area. Sometimes it was the other plants. We had a list of five other groups – by the time we had seen all five, we had found begonia.

When it was Saturday, I expected another trip to the forests, but my hosts were not prepared to go. I was baffled. I had worked seven days a week since I had been a student, for at least the past twenty years. Sometimes I went home early on Sundays and slept in the afternoon, but otherwise, every day was for work, because it was such a privilege to be able to do science, so interesting, and there is always so much to do. I never understood what it was that other people spent their time doing. Anything but science seemed so boring. But I was totally dependent on my hosts in Umtata, and they worked five days a week.

Within a month of my arrival, I had found plants easily in many places. In each one, the plants were unique, and there was far more variation than had been reported previously. The forests were largely intact and well protected, and the people friendly and helpful. I spent a night with two other women trying to sleep in a guard's hut at a forest station. There seemed to be ticks everywhere, and the two men guarding us talked loudly all night, smoking dagga. I spent a rainy day in a small house with a German woman and a South African botanist debating whether evolution had ever happened. I went collecting with a renowned amateur botanist I had written to before arriving. Tall, fit and with long legs, he seemed to enjoy being physically superior to academics interested in the plants he knew about. Elize had warned me that she took six months to fully recover after a day with this fellow, and I swore I would do better than that. I tried to keep up, but I tumbled down a slope at one point, and twisted my ankle at another time, and it was two years before my ankle was fully recovered. He did find one of the places where he had collected begonia before, and when I asked him what other species were in the area, he dictated twenty species' names to me.

A friendly and helpful man who was working for the Forestry Department of the Transkei government took me to several interesting forests. He liked to drive fast and let his bakkie skid on the gravel. We spent a night with an old friend of his, who had built a trail into the forest, at the coast, at the mouth of the Qora River. Our host was generous with his food and wine, and when I woke the next morning, I took the only creative photographs I made during that whole trip – pairs of neon coloured grasshoppers on huge heads of flowers, reflections of palm leaves in the quiet waters of a lagoon. The forest guards who accompanied us collecting were puzzled by me pulling a few leaves off plants, and gave me the Xhosa name Nomifino because I looked like a girl gathering spinach.

Several people resigned from the botany department while I was there, and I was offered a position. It seemed the stuff of dreams, promising full-time research close to these wonderful field sites. What could be better than to be paid to continue this work? One of those who resigned was a British man who knew he was dying of AIDS. His wife had died a few months before. His old clothes hung loose on his body, and he had sores on his skin. He never said 'AIDS', out of fear that insurance would not be paid for his wife. Alice, who is from Uganda, knew. He went back to England after a few weeks to stay with his parents. He died a year later. There were no reverse transcriptase inhibitors in 1991. But there were denialists, including a lecturer in the medical school, who told his classes that this story about AIDS was just a white man's plot to keep blacks from reproducing. Don't use condoms, have lots of babies! I wonder where the doctors are who received instruction from him, if they are still alive.

By the end of March, my notebook carries the record that I had made 57 collections, acquiring leaves from 414 plants and seeds from 204 of them. My three months of fieldwork came to an end, and the job offer had not yet been made official. I was warned to expect that it might not come through. I went back to North Carolina, now warmer and in spring, and then on to Toronto, feeling privileged to work in a lab with great microscopes in the company of several women involved in similar research. The job offer from Unitra[1] did come through, in the form of many pages of fax.

I was hired as a research associate, pretty low down on the academic ladder, but an ideal position as far as I was concerned, because I did not teach undergraduates and could do research full time with sufficient support

doing research or heard him talk about his research. What had he worked on? I went and looked. Found the year. The volume number was right for the year, but the page number for the beginning of his reference was in the middle of an article by someone else. I looked in the index for the year. Not there. I looked in the indices for the previous year, the next year, more and more of them. The article in his CV was fiction. I told some of my friends, but could never face him with my findings. I continued to read *Science* and *Nature* and *Genetics* and *Evolution*; the only thing I ever saw him reading was *Reader's Digest*.

I continued to read *Science* and *Nature* and *Genetics* and *Evolution*; the only thing I ever saw him reading was *Reader's Digest*.

for the field work I wanted to do. Elize warned me that publishing would hurt me professionally, but I just could not believe her. Had the world turned upside down?

Every time I went to the US I came back with another suitcase full of books. I learned that book dealers who come to conferences do not want to haul books back with them, and that I could successfully beg free or very cheap copies if I went and spoke with them as they were packing. My office filled with the journals I had subscribed to. I bought a complete set of back issues of one of those journals.

We worked on a proposal to get funding for our new Honours programme. I asked everyone for CVs. The one from the department head listed a paper in the journal I had just acquired all those old issues of. I was curious because we never saw him

My plans for research included additional collections from the wild, measuring and comparing leaf shapes, growing the plants and doing crosses. And another project, off the main course of my research, but which seemed both feasible and sufficiently interesting to pursue. The begonias often had silvery spots on their leaves when the plants first grew from seed, or when they re-sprouted after the winter. There were a few places where the leaves had these spots for the entire lives of the plants, even when they were flowering. And in those places, some plants had spotted leaves and some had plain green ones.

It is of interest generally in evolutionary biology why polymorphism is maintained. One assumes there is something good and something bad about both types, and they are balanced by opposing selective pressures. The question of spotted leaves was also an

1. The University of Transkei.

interesting one, since the spots certainly looked as though they would reflect light, and these begonias lived at the edge of the lowest light levels in the forest and were poor competitors, so there must be something good about having spots that kept them common. I started a long-term study of plants in this forest, at the mouth of the Qora River, down the road from Willowvale, where there was a path through the forest. In addition to being able

cliffs and climbing trees, while I stayed on safe ground. He had good eyes and could recognize the unusual asymmetric leaves of begonia better than anyone else.

We started the project at Qora by labelling plants, finding many right along the path, others above it in the cliffs. We had a routine for these trips. Early in the morning we would meet, and I would drive the old Land

> Sometimes when a group sang Nkosi sikelel' iAfrika, a voice would shout 'One settler, one bullet' at the end, rather like 'Play ball' at the end of the Star Spangled Banner at a baseball game.

to follow the spotted and green plants through the growing season, it was an opportunity to observe the plants in one place over the growing season. I found a method for labelling plants, using plastic paper clips and Dymotape. A friend in the US sent me thousands of plastic paper clips; I still use them.

David helped me with this study, as with much of the plant collecting. He was the assistant in the herbarium, having been hired when another person in the department noticed his good attitude and his aptitude for work as a gardener, and suggested that he apply at the university. He was great to travel with, as he would politely introduce himself to the people we met, get information about roads or plant use, and often find that he shared relatives with the people. David is deeply religious, and we suspected his goal was to become a minister, not a botanist. But he was learning about plants, and was helpful and willing. Despite his tiny size, I knew that he knew he was protecting me on our many trips. He was strong, and capable of scaling

Cruiser on the national road to Idutywa, where we had to put in petrol, because the vehicle used a lot. Then down the gravel road to Willowvale, and the smaller gravel road to the coast. We saw children on their way to school and waved.

There were lots of albinos, and I would count them, and came up with a much higher frequency than has been estimated elsewhere. We did that trip once every two or three weeks for about six months, and again the following summer. I'm sure people got to see us as familiar.

Once we got to the coast, we would pull up in the parking area, and greet the man who ferried people across the river mouth. We went through the plants by groups, David counting leaves and calling out numbers, me writing them down. Number of leaves with mildew, number of leaves with holes, number of flowers, number of capsules. We saw the plants grow, get eaten, die from mildew. Powdery mildew is a fungus and a common problem with cultivated begonias. It occurs naturally, and I had seen it on another species that dies back at the end of the summer. What was surprising is that the plants with spotted leaves seemed to be less severely affected by mildew than those with plain leaves. Spotted plants grew more slowly and flowered later, but in the end produced about the same number of seeds as the green ones. Once we had this result, I decided to take data on these plants for another season, thinking more about sampling, and increasing the number of plants. During the second season, there was no effect of mildew. It remains intriguing, but a third season of biweekly trips seemed too much effort for something that might not ever produce a clear answer.

That little forest along the river remains for me one of the most magic places I have known. In September the clivias flowered, including pale yellow ones. There was a stand of *Stangeria*, a type of cycad, denser than I have ever seen anywhere else. The *Streptocarpus* (cape primrose) were huge and overgrew the puny begonia plants. We saw orchids, snakes, dassies and birds. The people who lived on top of the cliff would come down into the forest to collect plant material and to snare birds. Cattle came into the forest near the beach. But the intrusions seemed not to take much toll.

My fieldwork moved north into Natal in 1993, partly because I needed to sample in those areas, partly because the PAC frightened us away. The Pan Africanist Congress was a constant presence on campus, with many members, posters in many places, and their conference shortly before the 1994 election. Sometimes when a group sang Nkosi sikelel' iAfrika, a voice would shout 'One settler, one bullet' at the end, rather like 'Play ball' at the end of the Star Spangled Banner at a baseball game. But there was no laughter, just embarrassed silence, and glances in my direction to make certain I was not offended. There were PAC warnings of preparations for the big storm; there were threats against white women and children; there were military units training in the nature reserves and intimidating the guards.

I did not want my Unitra contract renewed. What then, at the end of six years? The future of the university was not certain, and it seemed wisest to get out before the whole place imploded. I saw an ad for a population geneticist, my field of specialty, at Wits. I was planning a trip to Wits anyway, and when I was there I called the head of department and then went to speak to her. She phoned after I got back with an informal offer. The formal offer came through the fax machine at the travel agent's office, open closer to Christmas than the university, which usually closed for four to five weeks over the holidays. So everyone knew, even what salary I had been offered.

When I told my department head, he said, 'You'll be able to buy a house.'
After one last trip to a remote area, where David and Elize and I camped in the rain and found only four begonia plants; the movers came to pack my things. They filled many boxes with books, both from my house and my office. They appeared again in Johannesburg a few weeks later, carried those boxes and unpacked them, but they did not put the books on the shelves alphabetically by author, as I always do. My field notebooks, starting with the orange one, went on a special shelf, separate from all of the others.

# ANALYST'S THUMB

SUSAN CHEMALY

Some people have a death wish. A long time ago, when I was twelve, Emma, aged nine and my sister's best friend, said to me, 'I swallowed a safety pin'.
I said, 'Was it open or closed?'
'Closed', she said. 'I opened it and pinned it through a slice of bread and then I closed it again and then I ate the bread.'
'Then you're OK, it will just go straight through and come out the other end.'

I thought that was the end of the matter but Emma was worried. She told my mother, who told her mother. She was taken to the doctor and X-rayed. The safety pin was closed (they

for human beings, only that for rats, and he had not swallowed enough naphthalene to kill the average rat. So I assured him that he would not die.

Another scene: Third year inorganic chemistry and the preparation of cobalt acetylacetonate. Cobalt acetylacetonate is a beautiful dark-green crystalline compound. It was nearly 5 pm. The worst experimentalist in the class was anxious to go home and so was I. 'What can I do? My cobalt acetylacetonate is still a bit wet.'
'Spread it out on a watch-glass and leave it to dry overnight.'

'I swallowed some naphthalene. Will I die?'
I wanted to say 'Only if you are a moth,'
but I bit my tongue.

gave her the X-ray photograph for a souvenir) and, in due course it passed through her and came out the other end. Her mother was, quite understandably, furious.

Fast-forward to a chemistry laboratory at Wits University and an experiment to determine depression of freezing point. A worried student came to me and said, 'I swallowed some naphthalene. Will I die?' (Naphthalene is the chemical used to make mothballs.) I wanted to say 'Only if you are a moth,' but I bit my tongue. Instead I asked, 'How much did you swallow?'
He showed me the amount and I weighed it – 0.2 grams. We then looked up the LD50 (the amount needed to kill 50 animals if fed to 100 animals). The book didn't give the LD50

'What happens if something falls from the ceiling into my precious compound?'
'Put the watch glass into your locker and close the door. It'll be safe there.'

Unfortunately, the student had neglected to tell me that the compound was not just a bit wet; it was extremely soggy. The next day I found Worst Experimentalist eating a green sandwich. He had carefully placed the sandwich (wrapped in waxed paper) on top of his cobalt acetylacetonate. I volunteered to buy him a replacement sandwich from the cafeteria but he turned down the offer.

In recent years the number of such incidents has escalated. I caught a student trying to pipette concentrated sulphuric acid. This is

★24

equivalent to sucking up Coca-Cola with a straw, except that concentrated sulphuric acid is about 1 000 times as acidic as Coca-Cola and much more corrosive. (A human tooth, when placed in Coca-Cola takes about an hour to dissolve.) Fortunately for the student concerned, concentrated sulphuric acid is very viscous and sticky and thus difficult to suck up into a pipette. I caught him before the acid reached his mouth.

Another student used hot methanol (one of the poisonous ingredients of methylated spirits) to extract the constituents of rooibos tea for analysis. He then felt thirsty and drank the brew.

A well-endowed student wore a low-cut mini-dress to her chemistry practical under her very skimpy laboratory coat. She prepared peroxyacetic acid in acetic acid (both of which are corrosive) in a beaker on her bench, not

experiments go wrong because of analyst's thumb than for any other reason.' I didn't know what he meant, so he explained. A volumetric flask, which is commonly used in chemical analysis, has a long thin neck with a small opening at the top. The opening is closed with a stopper. The opening is just the right size to accommodate a human thumb. A common error that students make, he said, is to put their thumb over the opening, turn the flask upside down and shake the contents vigorously. When they do this, whatever is on their thumb is transferred into the flask. This includes sweat and flakes of skin as well as any chemicals they may have previously touched, and is enough to spoil the results of an experiment.

Recently I noticed the best-looking young man in the third-year pharmacy class, with his little quiff of gelled hair sticking up in front and surrounded by his usual little

## She got such a fright when she smelled her preparation that she spilled three drops on her cleavage, giving three tiny measle-like spots.

in the fume hood as I had reminded her five minutes earlier. She got such a fright when she smelled her preparation that she spilled three drops on her cleavage, giving three tiny measle-like spots. She was in a frenzy of anxiety. By this time I was irritated. I told her to wash it off and informed her rather snappishly that she had fish and chips syndrome and that she would live. (The vinegar sprinkled over fast food fish and chips is simply dilute acetic acid.)

Long ago when I was a student, a wise old Analytical Chemist told me, 'More

entourage of female admirers. He had a volumetric flask containing a bright orange solution of potassium dichromate in his hand and he was shaking it vigorously with his naked thumb over the opening. At last! Analyst's thumb. I said to him, 'You're going to have a problem with analyst's thumb.'
'What's that?'
I explained. He shrugged. I tried again: 'When you are a pharmacist your customers are not going to like it if you shake their cough mixture with your thumb over the top of the bottle.'

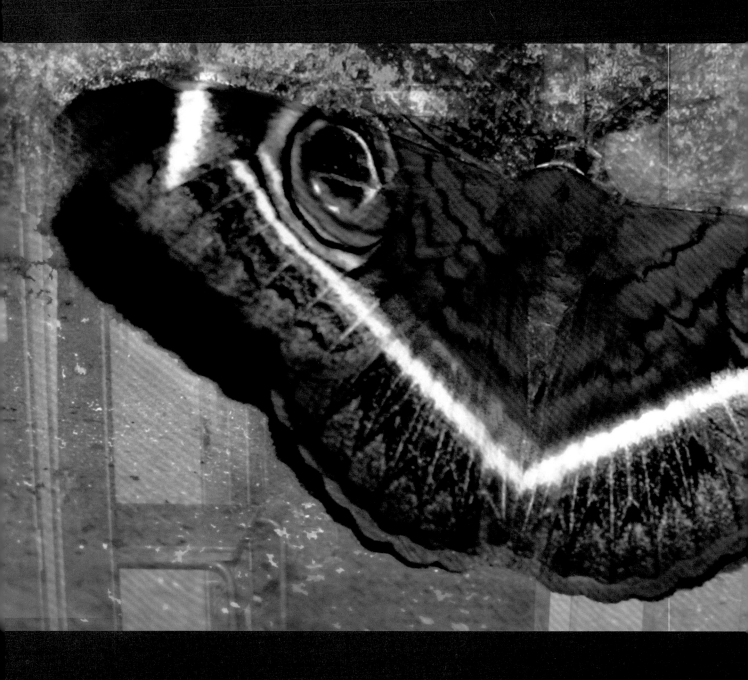

Another shrug. I fired my last shot,
'Did you know that potassium dichromate is
carcinogenic?'

A little later Gelled Quiff came to see me
in my office. He was holding his right hand
closed. He slowly opened his hand and
showed me that his palm and his fingers were
bright orange.
'How did that happen?'
'Well, you see I left my spatula at home so
I just thought I would take some potassium
dichromate with my hand and put it in the
volumetric flask. What can I do?'
'Wash it off with soap and water,' I said
rather brutally. 'You will probably need a
scrubbing brush.' I was about to say that
potassium dichromate was not a very potent
carcinogen and that the added risk of cancer
during his lifetime was probably tiny but I
stopped myself.

A student put a nice big piece of magnesium
in a flask and added concentrated
hydrochloric acid. He then put his eye to
the opening of the flask to see what was
happening. I threw him out of the laboratory.

A student came late to the practical so that
she didn't hear the instructions. Because of
this she accidentally generated chlorine gas.
When I had finished coughing, I threw her
out as well.

After 40 years of dealing with the death wish,
I'm getting hardened.

'Did you know that potassium dichromate is carcinogenic?'

SUSAN CHEMALY

# SERIAL NIGHTMARE

SUSAN CHEMALY

Last night I dreamed that it was the start of a new term at Wits. I had come back to work two days late and the second-year students had written a test in my absence. The test was on their first-year work and they had forgotten everything. The test paper was full of misspellings, grammatical mistakes and strangely mangled questions. I tried to mark the tests but I couldn't make sense of them because I couldn't read the students' writing. Some of them had Tipp-Exed out their answers and some were writing in code. Also, my red pen had evaporated. I tried to find out who had set the test but nobody could tell me. The students didn't know. The class representative suggested that it might have been a polar bear. I asked the secretary but she was talking on the telephone. While I waited, she turned into a squirrel and nibbled an acorn. I asked my colleagues but they couldn't hear me; they continued their headlong rush

wasn't worried about contamination because he made his coffee with distilled water. The Faculty said that everybody was on leave and anyway it wasn't in their job description. I decided not to ask the Vice Chancellor because he was too high up.

I wanted to ask my friend about the test but I couldn't find her. I could see her and another of my colleagues sitting in a lecture theatre crowded with students and staff. I tried to talk to her but there was too much noise. Somebody had set up an enormous distillation apparatus in the aisle. The lecture theatre was steeply banked and I wanted to go out the back door. As I climbed the stairs they grew taller and taller until I was pulling myself up using finger and toeholds. Suddenly, I was back in my office and the cleaner was emptying my wastepaper basket. There was a cloud of fruit flies and I was trying

## The Faculty said that everybody was on leave and anyway it wasn't in their job description.

along the corridors without opening their mouths. They were late, like Alice's rabbit. I realized that I had a bit of a problem when one of them ran right through me.

The department vanished in a puff of black smoke, leaving behind the smell of rotten eggs. I registered that the fume hoods weren't working (again) and one of the fourth year students was sloshing around with sulphuric acid. She said that she was just washing her glassware. The head of department was washing his coffee mug next to the student and in the same basin. He assured me that he

to shoo them away. I tried to close the window but it was too heavy and I was frightened that I might fall out in the process. It was eight floors to the ground and I had forgotten how to fly. I asked the cleaner, who had turned into a lioness, if she could clean my office but she said that she was sorry, she had to go and wash the wall of the lecture theatre.

Suddenly I was outside the Physics building sitting on the steps with a group of second year chemistry students. A chipmunk and a capybara were predicting the future careers of their fellow students. They awarded

PhDs to each other. They said that I might manage an Honours degree if I worked really hard. I walked round to the back of the Physics building. Then I was part of an audience in a tent. Our head of school was singing 'Don't cry for me Argentina' using an behind me and pinned three cartoons on the notice board. They were cartoons of me drawn by the students and I started crying. The baboon said that she was very sorry but she had suppressed the worst one because it was libellous. I was back in the lecture

## A baboon came up behind me and pinned three cartoons on the notice board.
## They were cartoons of me drawn by the students and I started crying.

old-fashioned microphone. She was backed by a small orchestra. The scene changed and I was lost on the Wits campus. There was a student with me and he was also lost. We were looking for the Senate House but somehow I knew that it had not yet been built. There was a swirling fog and it was icy cold. The scene changed again and I was in a conference room. The lights were off and someone was showing slides and talking incomprehensibly. There was an empty seat next to me. Sitting in the seat next to the empty seat was a seal with long whiskers. I was very pleased to see him. The lights went on and I was pinning an important notice on a big notice board. A baboon came up theatre. There was a big splash of black paint on the wall. The lioness was trying to clean it off with a pot scourer. She was having no success. She said that someone in the next door lecture theatre had stolen the chalk and the blackboard duster. Before I could reply, I was in a meeting. There was confusion, shouting and a mess because somebody had spilled a 100-litre drum of coffee on the table. I said the coffee was supposed to be locked up, but quickly retracted the statement because I remembered that I was muddling coffee and absolute alcohol. I pushed my chair over to create a diversion and all the chairs simultaneously fell over, hitting the floor with a loud crash. And then I woke up.

# GUIDELINES FOR SURVIVING A FULL SCHOOL MEETING

JANE CASTLE

1. Arrive late, looking harassed and preoccupied, and announce that you were held up by something far more important and urgent.

2. Complain that the agenda is overloaded and wasn't circulated sufficiently in advance. Persist in adding several items under 'General'.

3. Hold the floor as long as possible. Others' views are unimportant.

4. Scorn the contributions of younger colleagues and those who work in 'lesser' disciplines.

5. Insist that your input be acknowledged and honoured, not merely heard.

6. Remind colleagues of the illustrious history of the school, with the implication that this golden age will never be recreated with the current cohort of staff and students.

7. Resist invitations to join any working group or team, pleading a heavy teaching and assessment load.

8. When the meeting runs overtime, make loud, aggrieved complaints. Demand that your items top the agenda of the next meeting.

There are too many penises in the room.

# UNIVERSITY SPACES 1 AND 2

MARGARET ORR

SPACE 1: KILLING TIME ~ SHB1

We are in the Senate Hall basement. The room is crowded, latecomers sitting on the floor, crouching on the steps. The crowd susurrates, teeth and claws clacking; eyes avid with anticipation; pens whetted, their sharp points gleaming, poised to rip into notepads. Perched at strategic viewpoints, with hooded eyes and scraggy necks, are the members of the selection committee. It is the time of choosing. One by one, the candidates for Dean will be led before the rustling rows, and will tell us about their plans for the Faculty.

'Beware of Fans', a large sign reads behind the lectern where they will stand. An incongruous warning. I imagine loudly cheering panty-throwing teenage girls, chanting and singing along with particularly catchy refrains about postgraduate throughput rates, and sentimentally swaying and waving Bic lighters aloft at the chorus about Africanization of the curriculum.

But perhaps the sign refers to the metal-flanged variety? Perhaps there is a risk that the ceiling fans will become so violently agitated by too much hot air that they will start rotating ever more wildly, rip loose of their moorings and hurtle spinning into the air, whirling viciously into soft, exposed necks, splattering blood and clots of graying scholarly hair across the puke-green walls of the lecture room?

Either way, fans are to be wary of in this room, for they may disrupt this grave scholarly ritual – the time of hunting down the chosen one – the new Dean.

The first candidate talks about a university of beauty, here in the crowded dingy basement, with dangerous fans, soggy grey cement corridors, chipped and scratched lecture desks ('Bongi loves Tebogo desparatly X 100' is scrawled at my seat. 'Desperately' is misspelled. Perhaps they were mathematics students?) The second candidate makes jokes about being an American (he didn't vote for George Bush, he says) and offers the temptation of millions of dollars of potential donor funding. There are some questions. The serried ranks rustle and murmur, sometimes laugh – politely – at jokes, their teeth bared, the saliva gathering at the corners of their mouths. They dart looks at each other, roll their eyes, snort into their jowls, and paw their notes.

The candidates leave. The herd remains, to shred and sniff over the carcasses. There will be two more here tomorrow. And then smaller, more vicious packs – the Institutional Forum, Council – will enact the final ritual of choosing. And the Faculty will have a new Dean. The old one is just dry bones, now.

SPACE 2: MEETING ~ COUNCIL CHAMBER SH 11TH FLOOR

The room is full of men, weighty and hearty in the seats around the supposedly egalitarian oval table, and hanging on the walls in gilt frames and murky oils. It is the senior executive team's romper room. I am brought into the room, apprehensive and tentative, to discuss performance appraisal. My father used to remind me of Winston Churchill's advice to deal with nerves in front of an important audience. 'Imagine them all naked,' he recommended. Somehow, this advice doesn't work for me today. The portentous bespectacled faces around the table sit atop saggy, aging chests, dusted with curly graying hair, and below the gleaming surface of the table their variously scrawny or doughy buttocks squelch out over the seats. There are too many penises in the room – ten of them all told, some black, some white, squished against the plush grey of the expensive executive chairs. I feel simultaneously threatened and even more dangerously at risk of falling into an uncontrollable fit of 'church giggles'.

I have brought a 30-page document on performance appraisal to be discussed. But this was also not a good plan. I look around the room. One Dean is reading the newspaper, two are paging through their wad of meeting notes in a befuddled and distracted fashion, either looking for my document, or trying to do some advance homework on the next item on the agenda. Or perhaps they're just looking for something more interesting to read. The Registrar and the Executive Director of Finance are having a private conversation; one of the DVCs is inspecting his manicure. We wade through my document. They clearly haven't read it, but are impatient with my careful, diplomatic attempts to signpost them through the thinking without insulting them. They become solemnly transfixed by randomly selected words; get fractious and distracted by items which refer to previous decisions made, and query with great perplexity whether they ever actually decided these things; stare dubiously at figures and challenge the data-gathering methods. They page to and fro through the document (those not reading the newspaper or otherwise engaged) getting lost in each other's references to the third bullet point in section three halfway down page nineteen.

We are clearly headed for a decision to refer the document back for further revision.

A moment of inspiration strikes. In bright, cheery, motherly tones, I suggest we make paper planes out of the document. The Dean of Engineering is enthusiastic and sets to work on a turbo jet. The Dean of Science hasn't mastered scissors yet, and wails in petulant frustration. I hand out crayons and finger-paint and the DVCs squat happily on the floor making jubilant splashy handprints all over their agenda documents. One Dean has to be persuaded out of trying to eat the crayons, and the Registrar and Executive Director of HR get into a tussle on the floor. A generally productive and jolly time ensues, interrupted by Elias bringing tea and biscuits.

As they settle down in their seats again I leave the room to go back to my office to dredge up a previous version of the document to bring to them next time to keep them happy and distracted. The university's IR adviser is waiting outside for her turn to go in, to talk about wage negotiations and the leave liability. I raise my eyebrows at her, smile, and sigh.

'How was it?' she asks.
'Not too bad, today,' I say. 'At least the Executive Director of Finance seems to have stopped biting the others, and the Dean of Health Sciences' toilet training seems to have kicked in.'
'Oh good,' she sighs. 'I've brought them some flavoured playdough for my session.'
'Great idea!' I enthuse. 'We've got to keep them amused, or else they might try to run the university again.'

And that was another very good day on the heaventh floor at Wits.

'How was it?' she asks.

'Not too bad, today,' I say. 'At least the Executive Director of Finance seems to have stopped biting the others, and the Dean of Health Sciences' toilet training seems to have kicked in.'

'Oh good,' she sighs. 'I've brought them some flavoured playdough for my session.'

'Great idea!' I enthuse. 'We've got to keep them amused, or else they might try to run the university again.'

# KNOWLEDGE IS POWER, AND YOU'D BETTER BELIEVE IT

MARY RORICH

I've had plenty of unhappy times at Wits, believe me. Conflict with other staff members, fury at the misogynist mentality of the eleventh floor, frustration at the bumbling, slow, pedantic, ineffectual bureaucracy that hasn't changed in 25 years. But every day when I arrive on the campus, to the underbelly of the city; like a madam in a knock-shop, she watches equivocally the mess of city garbage tangled erotically with roadside gambling and sunglass-snatching, people spitting, urinating, lying down and dying. Through gray peepholes of sky or cement, Wits spies on the empty high-rise

> Wits is voyeur to the underbelly of the city; like a madam in a knock-shop, she watches equivocally the mess of city garbage tangled erotically with roadside gambling and sunglass-snatching, people spitting, urinating, lying down and dying.

driving through booms that won't open or won't close, edging around service vehicles reversing into un-navigable spaces, I feel my heart beat. Yes, this is home; this is where I want to be, where I belong. Where I feel I make a difference and where I feel the pulse of the nation getting stronger every day. Quite simply, I love Wits.

It's not a beautiful campus, like UCT[1] or Stellenbosch; not well-appointed like Tukkies[2]; even Rhodes seems to have more space to spread itself and proclaim its message. But Wits *is* the message: the steely truth of 'knowledge is power'. And you'd better believe it.

Situated on a ridge where the wind blows sharper than anywhere else in Gauteng (just warding off the smell of crime from Yeoville, Doornfontein and Hillbrow), Wits is voyeur

skyline at dusk, on the city sulking in the morning Soweto smog, on the city waiting to become, to be, to be pulled back into the snatch for land, on the city waiting for the new Cecil Rhodes, or Abe Bailey, waiting for Godot.... And Wits watches, and pretends to care, but the fences are up, and the turn-stiles and the glass booths, and when will they come down? (They weren't there when Wits was white.)

To the North, Wits smiles a gap-toothed grin, beckoning: To the Randlords, to the warm brick-and-bay Herbert Bakers pointing 'Yonder lies my Hinterland'; to the sprawling acres of Houghton, final prison of Nelson Mandela, its walls high with sweet peas, cannas, creepers and security. Around him, Wits beckons the last pieces of pink in Africa, those who host Michael Jackson, George

---

1. The University of Cape Town
2. The University of Pretoria

## The edge of what?  On the edge, over the edge, go over, find it, think it, let it fill you and make you bleed with desire.

Bush and Mark Thatcher, those (far too many) neo-colonials who have money and mummy. Way beyond, Wits beckons the new ones with their white-washed houses, kidney-shaped pools, four-wheel drives and painlessly negotiated democracy, with their 2.4 children and their kittens and puppies and house alarms and guns in the safe. Or not. And then Wits beckons the Magaliesburg, not easy to see through the city smog nowadays, but perfectly visible on a good day in 1926.

Yes, they are all in Wits' catchment area, and they come in their City Golfs or their baby Mercs, or by taxi or on foot, from the station and the highway, to the steely, ugly place to learn the steely message: 'Knowledge is power', and you'd better believe it. And then Wits grabs them, and guts them and they learn it's not at all about a fantasy mountain or a pretty little town with pot to smoke and sex to have; it's about the edge, 'Wits Gives You The Edge'.  The edge of what?  On the edge, over the edge, go over, find it, think it, let it fill you and make you bleed with desire. And then they understand. And their hearts beat, and they are happy and they know they have found it, the place, the thing; they have found their freedom and they have understood the steely message: 'Knowledge is power, and you'd better believe it'.

# STUDENT SURVIVORS[1]

MARY RORICH

Sibongile Morake is a second-year student who came into the foundation music course three years ago with no formal music knowledge, very inadequate English skills, but a real passion for vocal performance.

She is now an excellent singer, marimba player, participant in drama productions and a strong presence in the music division. During her first two years at Wits she lived in a flat in Hillbrow with a large number of other students and walked to Wits every day, often returning late at night because of her involvement in extra-mural activities. She was raped twice on her way home and is, as a result, HIV-positive.

She has had to have extensive counseling for post-traumatic stress and depression. Pressure from the music division gained her a precious place in a residence on campus; however, at the time of the subsidy cuts, the university changed her financial package to one paying fees only and she must herself find the money to pay her residence bill. Sibongile has a real fear that she may be forced to leave this 'safe' place.

Julius Matabane is the son of a single-parent, Katie, who has had to take early retirement because of poor health. She earned R400 a month in Middelburg until her retirement. Julius was raised by relatives because Katie was a very young teenager when he was born. He was not aware that the beautiful young woman who frequently came to visit was his mother, although he always felt he was an outsider to his 'adopted' family. During a family row when he was twelve, he discovered his relation to Katie and ran away to join her. His foster parents fetched him several times, but he was determined to be with his mother. Julius and Katie are still very close and Julius tries to find the odd bit of money to take home to her. He managed to educate himself while living in Middelburg, getting a below average Matric in his early twenties.

1. Names have been changed

Then he worked in a shoe shop, trying at the same time to save enough money to come to Wits as a mature student to study music. Julius lost his full financial aid package when the university subsidy cuts came in. He was forced to leave residence and 'squat' on the fifteenth-floor of University Corner, a hair with a plastic fork he picked up from the student canteen. Julius is now in third year, a painfully thin student whose only means of sustenance is the music division sandwich. He works incredibly hard at his academic and also music subjects. He has taken two full years of English and loves the great English

## He had to comb his hair with a plastic fork he picked up from the student canteen.

dilapidated, sometime condemned office block on the south-east corner of the Wits campus. He would press his trousers by spreading them out under the carpet and sleeping on them during the night. He had to be out of the premises every morning by 5 am before the cleaners arrived. The night before his first-year singing exam he arranged to sleep in a friend's room in residence; somehow the arrangement went awry and he was left without the change of clothing and even the comb he needed to make a good appearance (he is obsessively tidy). He had no option but to wear his clothes from the day before and comb his

classics, like *Pride and Prejudice* and *Wuthering Heights*. He has taken part in major dramatic and musical productions in every year of his studies, and has the general appearance – one which he consciously cultivates – of a Sophiatown journalist, muso or even gangster: wide trousers, spats and sometimes a broad-brimmed hat. He has not failed a course since he has been at Wits, despite poor matric results. He sings both opera and popular music and has a great on-stage presence. His dream is one day to be able to afford to bring Katie to Johannesburg to see him star in a musical or play.

MARGARET ORR

# IRON ORE

MARGARET ORR

What do you have to do to be a warrior? Sometimes it's really simple. You have to speak. Speak out into a silence. Speak when no one wants to listen. Speak when what you are going to say will be unwelcome; will be misheard; will expose you utterly to ridicule, to calumny, to anger, to public shame, to misunderstanding. Speak when the price of speaking is unimaginably high, but the price of silence is even higher.

You are an ordinary woman. A bit of an introvert. You like books, gardening, movies. You love your kids, you do your best to love your husband, you often don't feel quite grown-up enough to be doing the superwoman stuff of being a professor, running a home, managing birthday parties, your team, sibling squabbles and aging, ailing parents. You like to be liked. You like to see yourself as a peace-maker, gentle, caring, sympathetic, a voice of reason and sensitive compromise in heated meetings. You think you're a nice person. You believe you're pretty much a 'good girl'.

And then suddenly you find yourself having blundered into a zone where it's really dumb to have brought your vagina to work.

In 1999 I arrived on the Council of Unisa[1]. The youngest member apart from the student representatives. One of a handful of women in a room full of men. In the high-backed chair at the head of the room, the only seat fitted with a microphone, was the chairperson of Council – urbane, authoritative, in a bespoke shirt with monogrammed cuffs, his yellow Lamborghini with its vanity plate in the plum parking place below the council chamber windows. Skirted in pale leaf-green, surrounded by a wisp of *Angel* perfume (it was far too expensive to wear every day, but it accompanied me to Council meetings to give me confidence), I must have looked like easy prey. And the chairperson homed in on me.

The trip from safe, 'good girl' territory to the battlefield that asks you to become a warrior is a meandering one – the scenic route, perhaps? There are moments of ambiguity and discomfort, but you tend to ignore them, laugh them off, tell yourself you're imagining things. It starts with the jokes. The comments about what you're wearing or how you look. And then it moves to touching, to hugs. The drunken innuendoes. The hints at the disparity of power between you, and the vacant management positions coming up. The requests for meetings that seem – but surely they're not? – to be inching the interaction away from the professional zone into murkier, more loaded territory.

And then – suddenly – the scenic route ends at a precipice. It's an ordinary day, after an ordinary meeting, and you're waiting for the lift, and you are being groped and pawed and having a whisky flavoured tongue thrust into your mouth. And there and then your life changes. You can't play it safe anymore. But

1. The University of South Africa

still you try the ways you know, the strategies women use to deal with 'unpleasantness'. You write a letter. You appeal for professionalism and mutual respect. You point out – politely, tactfully (got to save his face, after all) – that the behaviour is unwelcome, that it makes you feel unsafe, that you want it to stop.

But it doesn't. And then you find out that it's been happening to other women. And you have a choice. You can run away, hide, resign. You can grin and bear it. You can even lie back and think of promotion to DVC. Or you can fight. You can stand up and speak. And somehow, from somewhere, the courage comes to make this choice. And the warrior rises. And you speak. What no one tells you (well, OK, they mention it vaguely, the way jolly childbirth books written by men warned you of the 'discomfort' of labour), is that this is not

## And then you find out that it's been happening to other women. And you have a choice.

enough. That finding your voice – once, however articulately – will not be the end of it. The belief that if you take a hard decision, if you embark on right action, the universe will somehow reward you for your courage by smoothing the subsequent path, proves woefully naïve.

What happened next was the stuff of tacky newspaper stories and *You* magazine articles. The students (my students) got a mangled version of the story. And – as students have been doing for greater and lesser causes since the 60s – they demonstrated. Toyi-toyiing on the steps of Unisa, they waved posters saying 'Margaret, give us a kiss'; 'Margaret Orr is a white racist bitch';

'Professor Orr is a slut'; 'Orr is using her womanhood to block transformation'. They read out a memorandum claiming that 'this white woman has shamelessly displayed her willingness to be used as bait in a racist plot' and calling for my resignation.

It was small consolation that many of the posters were misspelled, and that the memorandum was full of egregious grammatical errors. (This was no consolation at all, actually, since I had been teaching English as a Second Language, and writing skills, and the wonderful speeches of Shakespeare, for some years by then, and I would have hoped for more rhetorical elegance from my students.) The overriding sensation was one of public shame and humiliation. In a zone where I had striven to be utterly professional, a cortex on legs, I was stripped naked. My physical safety was threatened, my professional integrity was questioned, my morals and motives were interrogated, my job was at risk.

And so the battle was on. Like any academic, I handled the crisis with great warrior-like assertiveness. I did research. I read the Anita Hill and Tailhook transcripts. I perused dissertations and academic articles on gender issues in the workplace. I studied the Labour Relations Act, the Employment Equity Act, the Constitution. I did qualitative interviews with case study subjects and academic 'experts' on gender violence and harassment. Also, in less scholarly fashion, in the four years that the war waged, I took anti-depressants, started smoking, stopped eating or sleeping – much, started wearing black jeans and combat boots to work, cut my hair brutally short, and had the Chinese symbol for courage tattooed on my shoulder. And I wrote. Not the research articles or dissertations or conference papers that I should have, had I been properly focused on my career, but diary entries, long stream of consciousness raves, and (at last count) some 1 024 pages of legal statements and depositions.

Four years is a long time to keep the fire in your belly alight. The warrior armour becomes heavy and you long to put it down. And it is tiresome to have to keep reaffirming your choices. You're tired. You want to get on with your life. You

A black woman, a member of Council, a mentor, a respected intellectual, winner of an award for services to the women's struggle, buys me cappuccino, leans confidingly over the table at a chi-chi coffee bar and says 'You know, my dear, African masculinity is a frail thing. It needs to be propped up in these ways. We need to save his face. How much can we pay you to be quiet and go away?' (I'm a prop for African masculinity? That's why I spent ten years studying and working in academe?)

My spouse – exasperated at another day dealing with torrents of weeping and a crisis that has lasted so long that he's never going to get a turn at a crisis of his own – pleads 'Give this up. It's costing too much. You've made your

## Give this up. It's costing too much. You've made your point. It's time to walk away.

should be working on your career. You haven't published an article in months. Your marriage is crumbling around you. You're being a really bad mother. You look drawn, haggard, getting old beyond all the ministrations of Estee Lauder.

At almost every stage, the choice is offered you again, to run away, to give up, to return to ways of being that are known, comfortable, ordinary. And the serpents of temptation slither up to you again and again, and in many forms, enticing you to succumb to easier, safer options. Whispering that you are dumb, idealistic, foolish. That your cause is trivial and self indulgent. That your crusade is dangerous and will destroy your life.

point. It's time to walk away. This man's karma will get him.' (But what, – I ask – what if I'm his karma? If I, with all my resources, walk away from this, who will take on the fight?)

I'm driving in my car with my daughter. We are going to CNA to buy crayons for school. She is just learning to read, and we spell out the newspaper posters on the lamp-posts. We stop at a traffic light and she leans forward and says 'Mommy, what is that word?' I read out the poster – 'UNISA PROF KLA OOR GESOENERY'[2]. I falter, stop. 'But what does that mean?... Mommy? Why is your photo on the newspaper?' I fumble for my dark glasses, look away from the newspaper vendor who is thrusting my face at me through the window.

---

2. UNISA Professor complains about kissing.

ORR YOU ARE USING YOUR WOMANHOOD TO DERAIL TRANSFOR- MATION HOW DARE YOU

PROF IS BIT

MARGARET YOU ARE BEING USED YOU ARE NOW A SCRAP

BITCH

'I'M YOUR HUG!

MAGRET - I NEED

ORR

A

CH

BITCH'

PROF. ORR. YOU ARE PROMOTED FROM BEING A BITCH TO

ORR, PROF. ORR. YOU ARE PROMOTED FROM BEING A BITCH TO A WITCH

I explain, as best I can, in terms a six-year-old can understand, what is happening. We talk about OK touching and not OK touching, and your right to object. Her fascination with the new skill of reading evaporates in her escalating anxiety. 'But Mom, if the judge thinks you're lying, will you go to jail? And then who will look after us?'

I go down to the cafeteria – desperate for a break from my office where I've been holed up since the demonstration. (Actually, I didn't need a break, I needed a KitKat.) It is late afternoon, the cafeteria is almost empty. There are two women cleaners pushing their

guys look like you need some sweetness in your lives,' I say in amiable tones. And I leave, silence behind me. Climbing the stairs an undignified two at a time, I laugh with delighted power, but also – damn my over-developed academic critiquing voice – wonder whether I've now truly confirmed the version of white condescension and patrimony skewered in postcolonial writing.

I go to the department of Social Work to do a presentation. The head of department introduces me to the staff as 'Margaret Orr, the woman in the news.' Catching sight of my tight, pale face, he hastily adds 'Of course,

> They look at me, snigger, whisper behind their hands.
> I don't understand what they're saying,
> but I can guess.

brooms around in desultory fashion. And – in the corner – a table of young, black, male students. They look at me, snigger, whisper behind their hands. I don't understand what they're saying, but I can guess. The cleaners lift their tired heads and stare at me. One of them has a daughter studying my course. I have spent hours with her, going through *Lord of the Flies, Julius Caesar*, subject-verb agreement. I have given her free author's copies of textbooks I have written. The woman's eyes skid away from mine. She starts sweeping with great concentration. She is ashamed, embarrassed. I hesitate at the door. The sniggers escalate. I grit my teeth. I go to the counter. I buy ten KitKats. I march over to the student's table. There is consternation as they realize I am bearing down on them. They flatten against their chairs, eyes darting to the exit to assess the distance for a quick getaway. Leaning into the group, I put the KitKats down on the table. 'You

she's not here to talk about that today. She's here to talk about performance management.' 'Ah, but what kind of performance?' interjects a professor from the back row, and his colleagues snort and splutter into their hands.

A female academic colleague from another university writes a letter to the press, quoting Africanist feminism, and asking what a middle class, designer-outfitted white woman thinks she is doing grandstanding such a trivial issue when her black sisters are being raped and brutalized in far more dramatic fashion. Another black woman, young, scared, meets me anonymously in a dark hotel bar far away in an erstwhile homeland. She twists and shreds a crumpled Kleenex in her hands, and tells me about a night in a hotel room, her hand forced into an open pants zipper. Tearful, overwrought, she and I and my lawyer giggle helplessly at her description of the 'small, soft, squishy thing' she encountered there. We imagine the devastating impact of such testimony in court. Fight them where it hurts, we cackle. But then she wipes the wet off her cheeks, and whispers urgently: 'I can never speak. He will kill me, or my mother. He will see to it that I never work again. You should be careful. He is a powerful man. If he knew you were talking to me... did you park your car in the hotel parking lot? It's the white BMW with Gauteng plates? It's been noticed... You are brave. I am not.' Driving back to Johannesburg in the pitch black godforsaken darkness of the African bush, the lawyer's BMW loses a tyre. We slew across the road and come to a stop in the ditch by the side. Roadside assistance arrives two paranoid hours later and tells us the tyre has been tampered with.

My son comes home from school, flushed,

The opposing lawyer argues that my case is vexatious and venal. 'Margaret Orr has said,' he declaims, 'that she wants an apology and is making a moral point. But we know,' and he leers around the court, 'that what she's really after is money, a lot of money. And I need to ask the court,' he pauses, impressively, adjusts his silk advocate's bib, '... what part of her body and dignity remain uncompensated for at this stage? What part of her body must we pay her for?'

What is it that keeps you going, on such a long, weary, complicated fight? What you begin to realize, with exhausted incredulity, is that the price ticket of any crusade is not always at the door. Like some nightmarish building project run amok, the costs keep mounting. What helps you sustain so expensive a battle for so

## What is it that keeps you going, on such a long, weary, complicated fight?

furious, embarrassed. His friends have read the *You* magazine article. All day long the school playground has ricocheted with shouts and taunts – 'Luke's mother kisses kaffirs!' And other things. Verbal volleys that he is too ashamed to tell me. He asks 'Mom, do you really have to keep doing this?'

I come to Wits, having fled my home university. I meet my new boss, the DVC, a black man. He says: 'Unhappy business, that Unisa thing. Are you sure it wasn't just a cultural misunderstanding? Surely now that you're at Wits you should drop it? It won't do you any good, here, you know.'

I'm sitting in court, listening to arguments I don't understand about *res judicata* and the vaguely obscene-sounding *facta probanda*.

long? It's not – curiously enough – anger and the desire for revenge. They are hot fuels, but they burn out fast and are cold ashes over the long months of waiting, hours sitting on hard court benches, tedious piles of paperwork. Some of what keeps you going is sheer bloody-mindedness. Some of it is the inexorability of a process that – once started – you cannot stop. Most of it is the other women who entrust their stories to you. Their stories testify to what begins to seem like a global terrorist war against little girls, against young, pretty women, against ordinary middle-aged mommies, against our grandmothers and aunts and sisters and daughters.

And then there is my oldest daughter. She is studying English, at Rhodes, and the stories have spread on the student network to sleepy

MARGARET,
MARGA

ROF. ORR YOU ARE
PROMOTED FROM

Grahamstown. She is reading *The Crucible* and reminds me how the hero refuses to sign a lying document that will save him from execution. She says, 'Remember Mom, when they asked him why, he said – "Because it is my name." ' And she says, 'I am so proud of you.' And so the war wages on, through four years of internal university processes, mediation, arbitration, the CCMA, the High Court, the Labour Court. And finally, finally, it is over. And the settlement feels like a triumph. The much-contested money will go to a bursary for young black women. For Angelinah, the daughter of the cafeteria cleaner, and others like her. It's called (I cannot resist a small moment of selfishness) 'The Margaret Orr

NEED

MARGARET YOU

RET YOU ARE BEING USED

PROF. ORR YOU AF

Women's Empowerment Award' – because it is my name.

So am I a warrior? Am I still a 'good girl'? I have failed myself and others and the cause in many ways. I have lost a marriage. I have made some hurtful choices. I have damaged lives – my own, my children's, my husband's, the Chairperson's and that of his spouse and children. I have been weak. I have done a lot of crying. I've had to fake courage in times when the real thing deserted me. But I spoke. In the face of wrong, I was not silent. And that is all. And that is – perhaps – enough.

Cool head scarf for bad/lazy hairdays

Lady's sun hat with flower

daisy power

Spring posy

Oh-so-pretty skirt and blouse

Bohemian

Polka dot purse

tassled Indian handbag

hippie skirt

Teacher's apples

Grandma's pearls

The responsible option

Grass-soled slip-ons

Ms. Professor

Mmm... What shall I wear today?

Tight t-shirt

Mama Africa

Bad girl

Head wrap

Traditional African print

'Don't mess with me'

'Notice-me' fitted jacket

fishnets for an easy catch

Ooh la la

Pencil Skirt

Killer corporate boots

mmm... After hours?

Emerald green snake skin (Pleather)

Bobby socks

Graduation gown

★53

TRACY MCLELLAN

# A FEELING FOR FABRIC — MY PERSONAL REFUGE

TRACY MCLELLAN

I taught myself to sew when I was about twelve. I received hand-me-down clothes from the daughter of a friend of my mother's. Selma Wilson was tall and thin (the way I was supposed to be but was not), and her clothes were a special version for slim girls.

I took them apart stitch by stitch, piece by piece, and then put them back together again on the old treadle sewing machine in the basement. A model from before 1914, it had long narrow bobbins and you ran it by making your feet tip up and down on the treadle. I don't remember if I ever wore any of the remade clothes but I remember my fascination with the geometric puzzle of how two-dimensional pieces of certain shapes were joined to make something three-dimensional.

Shopping for clothes with my mother at the beginning of every school year was torture. We looked for the 'Chubette' range of clothes, a huge embarrassment to begin with, and in our small town there was little variety.

The frustration of clothes shopping and the concurrent anxiety about the money being spent was then blamed on my abundant figure, and more simply on me. Sewing in the basement, creating something valuable from almost nothing, was a retreat from that battle and it felt liberating. I could be in control, and I could create things that would fit, and I would not be blamed for things that were not really my fault. I spent hours struggling to get the treadle machine to produce stitches, trying to get those old clothes into another form.

My parents gave me a sewing machine for Christmas when I was thirteen. They gave my brother a new French horn. The first garment that machine made was the kilt my brother made for himself. (He played the French horn professionally for a while but has given it up. Now he plays the bagpipes and has a custom-made kilt.) The machine did straight stitches and a simple zigzag. It had an attachment for buttonholes. It was portable, and I took it with me when I went to university. It travelled to every different place I lived, every dorm room, to my summer job at a hiking lodge, the apartments and houses I lived in as a graduate student. I would make at least a few things every year, a nice dress for Christmas or a skirt to wear to a conference.

When I was an undergraduate, part of the four percent of students who were female at a university 'polarized (student protestors rephrased it as 'paralysed') around science and technology', I took rare breaks away from studying and visited fabric stores. On a winter morning, it was one step in from the icy air outside to the heated inside, to a world of wonder, possibilities, creativity. The colours ranged from bright and loud to dull, subdued, subtle. I'd walk around slowly, looking at every bolt, feeling the material with my fingers, scrunching it in my hands to test it for wrinkling. The textures varied from soft, silky, velvety, fluid, to spongy, crisp, or stiff. Many fabric stores, like fabrics, have distinctive smells. Old ones smell dusty and mouldy; newer stores with natural fibres can smell herby and fresh, and cheap fabric stores filled with polyester smell like plastic.

My grandmother died before I started sewing,

but my father told me she always had a needle in her hand.

The print patterns on fabrics were endlessly fascinating. Bold geometric prints with colours interweaving, abstracts, florals. I would go to Harvard Square to upmarket *Fabrications*, to downtown Boston to the old, elegant shops, to Chinatown where there were cheap fabrics a student could afford.

Fabrics hold so much potential, so many possibilities. I would see a beautiful fabric, and the first thought was, what can I do with it? I made some bizarre clothes, like the long cape with a heavy lining that weighed a ton but still did not keep out the winter wind, a bathrobe of print corduroy, short orange

and buy nothing, just to worship in the shrine of beautiful fabrics. Sadly, the last time I was there I saw they have cut back their fabric section because the profit is higher in other things and people don't sew much any more.

I have moved many times and in each new city I got to know the fabric stores. In each new house, I found a space for cutting fabric, for the machine and the ironing board. Salt Lake City had a lot of fabric stores but not much variety, so I developed the habit of looking for fabric when I was travelling. San Francisco has great fabric stores; I found batiks in Trinidad. My old sewing machine was replaced with a

## My back was turned to the people I had a hard time feeling comfortable with, and my attention was turned to the patterns I could create.

velvet culottes, quilted bell bottom pants. I developed a strong preference for wearing skirts and dresses because they are much easier to make and fit than pants. When I struggled with my studies and questioned whether I was capable of finishing my PhD, I took comfort in my ability to create garments, to take a flat piece of fabric and make it into something wearable, and to escape from the academic world into one where there was room for creativity, where there was some reward and not just criticism.

I first went to Liberty of London when I was seventeen, over Christmas of a year I spent in France after high school. Liberty makes beautiful prints on fine cotton and silk, and the old Victorian building with its upstairs gallery provided an elegant backdrop. I cannot count the number of times I have visited Liberty, like a pilgrimage, every time I have been in London, sometimes just to look

new one in its own cabinet, and for a while I had a little room devoted only to sewing. On two occasions, I have spent a year in England, and each time, I bought a sewing machine there and continued sewing. When I went to Toronto to work for six months, I drove there in a small car filled with, among other things, my sewing machine.

I moved to Umtata with an electrical transformer so that the sewing machine would run despite the difference in voltage. My fieldwork around Port St Johns led me to Pru and her beautiful fabrics made with light-sensitive dyes and leaves, in rich colours. The combinations of purple and turquoise, both colours mixed of other colours, were intense and irresistible. I made dresses and curtains and bedspreads. I took the scraps and sewed them together to make patchwork. I cut long strips of fabric, then sewed them together to make another sheet of fabric, cut that at

> I took a course in tailoring, so I could make suits in the hope that the grey men in charge of the university would take me seriously.

an angle, sewed the pieces together again, making patterns of colour that had patterns inside them. My back was to the door of the cramped bedroom that held my single bed and the sewing machine cabinet; my back was turned to the people I had a hard time feeling comfortable with, and my attention was turned to the patterns I could create.

I read books about patchwork quilts and made a traditional Amish nine-patch pattern, an iterative, repeating pattern, like those I was thinking about in the formation of begonia leaves, with small elements repeated, forming similar shapes that are larger. When I finally got my own place to live and unpacked the quilts made by my grandmother, I found one in the same pattern, almost identical in size to what I had made. My grandmother died before I started sewing, but my father told me she always had a needle in her hand.

When I was little, we visited her in Maine every year, and received new quilts and bedspreads, and once a crocheted American flag made from tiny thread. For a while I had one of her quilts hung on a wall, hexagons made with triangles of a solid colour at the centre, and strips of print fabric surrounding the middle in several layers. I would look at it for hours, trying to see how many times the prints were repeated. There were a few that showed more than once, but hundreds of different fabrics, taken from other projects, from old clothes, were represented in that quilt. As a geneticist, I wonder whether there is some aspect of this love for sewing that can be inherited. My father had the culturally acceptable male version, doing cabinet work and making most of the furniture in our house.

Shortly after I moved to Johannesburg and started working at Wits, I took a course in tailoring, so I could make suits in the hope that the grey men in charge of the university would take me seriously. I made a grey suit and a bright red one, and another out of Italian linen that wrinkled terribly, and winter coats for the cold weather. My favourite suit, though, is made from a restrained African print, a combination from different sources – as we all are – that works successfully in the end.

Through all of my moving around the world, there have been two things constant in my life, science and sewing. I write and talk about the former a great deal. Fabrics, sewing machines and the creative process involved in making clothes have been with me as companions for many years, but not as something I talk about much or share with anyone else. My sewing is the source of most of my clothes, and they are somewhat more interesting and more luxurious than what I might be able to buy, but I don't sew just to make clothes. I love the rituals of choosing fabric, thinking about design, cutting fabric, sewing the seams, pressing. I try new things all the time, take courses if I can find them, read magazines. I enjoy thinking about the potential of what can be made, the choices I can make in matching fabric to design, in modifying patterns, creating something new. It is my retreat from the busy, competitive world of science, my refuge.

# THE BEGINNING OF ABSTRACTION

SIGRID EWERT

1966. I start primary school in Vereeniging, a gritty town spawned by the steel-manufacturing industry. I have learnt to read and devour one book after the other. When I have finished my weekly quota of books from the school library, I beg my Dutch friend who attends an English school for any book that she can spare, or turn to the books of my older brothers who have started school in Germany.

I become anxious – what will I do when I have read them all? The world is so old, surely all stories have been written, all songs composed? My mother laughs, 'No, there are always new ones being created.' I am not convinced, but cannot argue.

At school I learn grammars for three languages. I know the rules very well. I like rules, they tell you what you may do and what not. My vocabulary is large and I am proud of every word that I can add to it. I discover the pleasure of combining all my words strictly according to the rules, but in ways that no-one has ever done before. Only decades later will I understand that even if there are only a finite number of objects and a finite number of rules, the variations can be infinite.

At school I also learn to hide my knowledge from other children, and from most teachers. I soon learn not to speak much at all. I discover a series of books about children of the world, heavy green volumes with gold lettering. Carrying them home from the bus stop together with my satchel and sports clothes is not easy. Sometimes I leave the sports bag at home and pretend to have forgotten it. I learn not to hear the abuse of the teacher.

Patiently I work my way through all the volumes. I read folk tales from an Africa that I never encounter. I read about the life of a blonde German girl in the country where I was born. I wonder how my life would have been if my parents hadn't emigrated.

In the volumes on Asia I learn about the art of batik in India, how a woman works for many years with wax and dye to create a dress. I also read about arranged marriages. I am horrified. I realize that there is only one way to avoid marriage – I must find a way to be financially independent. I don't know any woman who is.

I also realize that I must not drop out of school.

As the years progress, I learn the rules of arithmetic, algebra, trigonometry. They are very simple and I don't spend much time on mathematics. I usually get full marks.

In my second but last year at school the headmaster announces an opportunity to take computer studies as an additional subject. I am immediately interested, hoping that it

I realize that there is only one way to avoid marriage – I must find a way to be financially independent. I don't know any woman who is.

The teacher has to spend most of her time cajoling and prodding the 30 boys in the class who can rely on job reservation for their future income and don't need an education.

will relieve the tedium of every day. However, the course is offered in Potchefstroom, a university town where they have one of the few mainframes in the country, and we have to arrange our own transport. I investigate the possibility of taking a train, but am disappointed. I encourage other pupils to take the course, so that the burden of transport may be shared among many. Two other girls show an interest.

Once a week after school we embark on a journey of one hour, the street cutting through mealie fields, the yellow monotony punctuated by the occasional grey silo. It is hot in the car

She has a difficult task. In the previous year the pass rate in mathematics of the matriculants had been very low. Even pupils who routinely got distinctions in all subjects hadn't done very well. Apparently the teacher concerned had dedicated most of his time to the first rugby team.

The new teacher has to ensure that the school doesn't get another such blow to its pride. She gives us many pages of homework. She also gives us the task of finding exercises of our choice and working out the solutions. My ego compels me to choose the starred problems at the end of each chapter. The teacher has to

I don't care much for people, even when they are well-behaved and healthy.

and the fizzy drinks and pies we have for lunch make me slightly nauseous. The lesson lasts three hours, and we only get home after six. Our parents have to take time off work to drive us there and we always feel guilty.

The class is attended by pupils from other schools in the region. Judging by the medals on their blazers they are all high achievers and I feel intimidated. I'm relieved when I am top of the class after the mid-year exam.

At school we have a new teacher for mathematics. She is tall and slim with dark, shoulder-length hair. If a French film had ever come to town, I could have compared her to Fanny Ardant.

spend most of her time cajoling and prodding the 30 boys in the class who can rely on job reservation for their future income and don't need an education. However, sometimes she can spare a few moments to look at my work. I begin to develop an interest in the subject.

Finally my last year at school arrives and with that, the application forms from university. I have to make a decision. I have no interest in medicine or law – I don't care much for people, even when they are well-behaved and healthy. Literature and science hold the balance. I weigh inclination with heavy facts. I have always liked reading and writing; have even won prizes in essay competitions. However, I must be financially

independent. If I decide to study in the humanities, I would have to be exceptional to get a post at a university, and I certainly don't want to teach at a school. On the other hand, my marks in computer studies have been consistently good. Skills in that new area are so scarce that a woman, even with average ability, has the chance of a career with a good income. My decision is made.

believe it is due to his broken Afrikaans, but even when he switches to English, the problem remains. I go through my notes again and again, but see no structure. In desperation I go to the library, find a shelf in a dark corner with a smattering of books about the subject. The books are old, but have not been used by many. I take a couple home, read a section in one, a paragraph in

## I cannot find a job for months and learn to survive on one loaf of bread and six eggs a week.

1979. I am in my second year at university in Stellenbosch, a pristine town of white buildings with red roofs in streets lined with huge oak trees. In the new semester we start with a course on formal languages in computer science. It is taught by an aloof lecturer with a PhD in physics from Cambridge, emphasizing his Britishness with his necktie.

My classmates and I are lost. Initially we

the other, finally find one that appeals to me. I read the introductory definitions over and over, try to follow the examples. Slowly it all begins to fall into place. In the exam I fly. The lecturer congratulates me; I am too surprised to reply.

1983. I arrive in Bonn, eager to study towards a *Diplom in Informatik*. I discover that my German is outmoded, and that

the promised financial support will not materialize. I discover that many take it for granted that I am a racist, because I have a white skin and come from South Africa. They don't ask me for my view.

When I mention to other students that I already have two degrees in computer science, they burst into laughter and

my fellow-students throw in the bin. I crave fresh food and pick berries that grow wild near the railway line. I wonder how one steals food from the supermarket without being caught; I don't have the courage to try.

While my body-weight dwindles, my mind comes alive. I learn what I can. I soak up knowledge and culture and let no experience

## I wonder how one steals food from the supermarket without being caught; I don't have the courage to try.

ask if there are computers in Africa. My indignation turns into helplessness when I attend lectures on formal language theory or commutative algebra and we cover in two hours what we had done in a semester in Stellenbosch.

I cannot find a job for months and learn to survive on one loaf of bread and six eggs a week, staring with longing at the food that

pass me by, provided it costs nothing. I also learn how to find jobs. I clean the house of a woman who lives with a number of cats and spends the whole afternoon smoking and drinking sparkling wine. I spend a day stamping letters for a business until my arm hurts so much that I cannot lift it. I work full-time for six months in different factories, repeating the same movement for eight hours every day and trying to avoid the spite of

co-workers for whom the factory is not just a stepping stone to a better post. I work in the kitchen of the diplomatic school with huge cauldrons of fatty meat soup during a heat wave, fighting back the nausea. Finally I am lucky and find a job at a translation bureau that specializes in the translation of software manuals. My German improves dramatically and with that, my self-confidence.

I don't neglect my studies completely. Systematically I complete my coursework and exams. I am ecstatic when I obtain the best possible mark for my dissertation, and simply incredulous when I get the same mark for the exam in commutative algebra.

1993. I am offered a post as research assistant at the University of Cape Town, with the option of registering for a PhD. My would-be supervisor encourages me to apply for funding with the Foundation for Research Development. My application is rejected. He smiles and says that it would have been granted if I were deserving, then suggests I apply through another programme.

At the weekly meetings he often makes offensive remarks, challenging me with a look to object. One day I do. The next day he informs me that he has called the funding body and withdrawn my application. I respond that I'll find another supervisor.

I make some enquiries, and am referred to a highly-rated professor of mathematics in Stellenbosch. I balk at the thought of returning to the village, but want a doctorate in computer science, simply for the prestige. We discuss possible topics for the thesis. He suggests formal grammars for picture generation. I have never heard of the existence of such grammars, but he has been

described as the best supervisor one could have, and I decide to trust him.

He asks me what type of pictures I would like to generate. Various possibilities flit through my mind – cancer tumours, fingerprints, faces for security. They don't appeal to me. I suggest patterns on textiles. He says that I could then write an article for a women's magazine. I'm taken aback by the remark. Judging by his smile, he is embarrassed too.

1995. I move to Stellenbosch and register in the department of computer science. They refuse to provide me with a computer; my supervisor borrows one in his department for me. They promise me a proper work space, but give it to a Masters student. Often when I get to my space in the open-plan office, there is rubbish lying on my desk. One day I find a curly hair in the middle of my keyboard.

I learn how to use Maple, a mathematical programming language. It is designed to solve equations, to integrate and differentiate, but it can also be coaxed into reading a grammar and creating an image that obeys the rules of that grammar.

My supervisor goes away for a couple of weeks. I use the time to play with the program and experiment with various grammars. When he returns, I show him the images. 'B-e-a-u-tiful', he says, 'I expected these grammars to be powerful, but never would I have imagined this.' We have coffee and carrot cake in celebration, tracing the pattern on the mosaic table.

We work on our first paper. Many new concepts need to be defined, then tested for soundness. It is exhausting. I am thankful if a term comes ready-made. For example, the set of pictures generated by a grammar is called a language. He is very quiet for a few minutes. '"Language" is a well-worn term, but doesn't quite fit. Why don't we call it a gallery? After all, we are talking about pictures.' I look at him in surprise. That is out of the ordinary. I see rows of men from the serious North reading that and finding yet another reason for dismissing a paper that comes from the Other Hemisphere, the Other Gender. I taste the word, frown, then nod.

It is Christmas. A friend asks me if I could look after her house in Cape Town during the holidays. I would love to, but the paper needs to be completed by the middle of January for submission to a conference. I spend day after day at the office, battling with theorems and word processors that do not want to do what I want them to, while the silly season comes and goes. At the beginning of January my friend calls me. Two men had broken into her house and raped the woman who stayed there in my stead.

my dusty sandals. I feel rather scruffy, even compared to tourists who must have been living out of suitcases for a while. The bicycle chain has left a mark on my leg.

I start looking at the displayed objects. Masks, pots, the usual wire art. A case draws my attention. Golden knives and spoons with red or blue patterns in the handle. Some jewellery. I have never cared much for jewellery, the weight of the chain around the neck, the jarring jangle of bracelets, the ring that irritates with its unavoidable click against the keyboard. Presents by well-meaning friends or relatives languish in a box or are nailed to the wall.

Then again, I have never seen jewellery like this before. There are two brooches, one a square and the other a triangle, both a play of gold and red. The triangle is lopsided, golden with five smaller fuzzy-shaped triangles in subdued red, approximately of the same size. If it contained another such shape, one

> I see rows of men from the serious North reading that and finding yet another reason for dismissing a paper that comes from the Other Hemisphere, the Other Gender.

A few months later I receive a blunt e-mail stating that the paper has been rejected. We decide to send it to an international journal instead. It is weekend. I cycle to the centre of the village in the blinding heat, stop and chain my bicycle to a lamppost. I have noticed the gallery before, strategically placed on the way to one of the oldest churches in the country. No tourist could miss it. I go inside, relish the cool and darkness of the old building with its thick white walls. The floorboards creak under

could call it an artist's interpretation of the Sierpinski triangle. The square is divided in horizontal stripes of equal width.

Both are elements of infinite sets of pictures that cannot be generated with a context-free grammar. When you are developing one triangle, you need to know how big the others are. When you are creating one stripe, you must be able to see how wide the others are. When you want to place a noun in a

> I think of that little girl who was so envious of those who may stamp their name on the binding of a book, or write it above a story. Now I am one of them.

sentential form, you need to know which verb has been chosen, because a ball can certainly not catch a dog.

I enquire after the price. Each brooch costs more than my monthly budget for food. All I can take away with me is a tiny spoon, and the hope that no-one shares my taste in jewellery. Then at least I can return regularly and look at my brooches.

A letter from a journal arrives. 'We have the pleasure of informing you that your paper has been accepted.' I read it over and over again. I think of that little girl who was so envious of those who may stamp their name on the binding of a book, or write it above a story. Now I am one of them.

I must find a way to commemorate this. The triangular brooch comes to mind. I cycle again to the gallery. The brooch is still there, and it is still very expensive. My upbringing doesn't allow me to spend so much money on such a frivolous object. I return home.

Two days later I buy it.

Another Christmas. The town is empty, except for me and the builders that want to put up a building in time for the return of the students with the deep pockets. The noise of the drills drives me out of my home early in the morning and I cannot go back until late. I have only my office to go to. I think and stare and eat. I am searching for a gallery with a particular characteristic. From one picture to the next the number of shapes must increase

as in the gallery of Sierpinski, but they must also become more intricate. I cannot imagine what that could be.

Suddenly the gallery presents itself. It all starts with three innocent dark squares on a diagonal. Each subdivides into four and spawns four squares on the new diagonal. In the third picture there are already five on each diagonal. Quickly the shapes become so small and many that the individual cannot be detected anymore, literally dissolving before the eye. I name the gallery after the trail of smoke left by an airplane.

I spend the next few days developing the grammar and creating the images. Everything is ready for the next paper.

After four years and six papers in international journals, I send my thesis to the external examiners.

Hugely relieved, I go on a short holiday with a friend. My body doesn't seem to share my happiness. I put it down to the stress of many months, and visit a doctor reluctantly. She diagnoses cancer.

A few weeks later I receive news that my application for a postdoctoral scholarship has been successful. I am determined not to let that opportunity pass me by and stoically accept seven months of surgery, chemotherapy and radiotherapy. In the long mornings at the hospital I read travel guides, looking up occasionally to watch a cockroach scuttle by. I also do my oral defence, prepare

# The world recedes

but the patterns stay

the final version of my thesis and write a conference paper.

1999. Winter has arrived in Bremen, a quirky city in northern Germany. I have just bought a camera with a part of my scholarship, the camera I have coveted for so many years. It is Sunday and I take the bus to Worpswede, a little village not far from Bremen. It is well-known for having been an artists' colony. The village still has many galleries and I intend visiting some.

It is a beautiful day, cold and crisp, but sunny. It is infused with the silence you find only in the North, where all automobiles are in perfect condition and the rules about noise are strict. I'm wearing a long coat in Prussian blue, a green scarf, gloves, well-worn leather boots. I am comfortable.

I want to stay outside, breathe the fresh air that blows from the ocean. I wander about, soon finding myself on the outskirts of the town. No-one talks to me, I don't have to talk to anyone.

I start taking photographs. I begin to notice patterns in the mown fields, in row after row of stubble in the subdued northern light. Patterns are in the leafless trees: dark branches against the sky, growing according to a simple, ever-repeating pattern. They are in the green moss on bark, sparkling with dew. In a front garden there is a flower, purple, each petal perfectly positioned. I'd like to take a photo, but I don't. I don't want to intrude. The world recedes, but the patterns stay. I photograph roof tiles, row below row, column next to column. I photograph a farm implement in front of the town museum, concentric circles, held together with spokes, each spoke ending in an outward pointing hook.

My great material is solitude;

and then in making the work, time....

Little by little

one gets so involved in the structure of things

that one forgets all the rest

and nature disappears.

That is the beginning of abstraction.

2001. Johannesburg. The sun throws a skewed rectangle on the wooden floor. Music plays. Boxes are scattered around the room. I have been appointed as Lecturer for Computer Science at Wits University and am settling into my new home. I unpack the brooches and rub them on my sleeve.

I teach formal language theory to third-year students and assume the responsibility for undergraduate coordination. A student asks

borrowed the communal kettle for half an hour for a meeting with class representatives, and she copies every mail to everyone in the School. I try to remember why I thought it would be worthwhile to undergo cancer treatment. I cannot.

My Honours student solves a problem that has been open for some time, and gets the best mark in the class for his research report. He wins a prestigious scholarship for PhD

## I receive anonymous e-mails. The senders claim to be students and state that they will rape and kill me if they find me alone.

me to repeat a complete lecture, because she has missed it; I refuse. A student tells me that he knows so little about a course that he sees no point in writing the exam, but wants me to give him the credit so that he can graduate; I refuse. A student asks me to go to the library and make photocopies of course material for him; I refuse. A student complains that my accent is so bad that he cannot understand a word in lectures. A student who is repeating my course complains that she has spent many hours a week in my office, receiving extra lessons, but still only obtained 74%, the third-best in the class.

I receive anonymous e-mails. The senders claim to be students and state that they will rape and kill me if they find me alone. I receive e-mail from colleagues, complaining about the noise that two students have made when walking through the passage and ordering me to ensure that it doesn't happen again.

I receive several long e-mails from a colleague: she complains that I have

studies in the United States. I am surprised that I can still share in his excitement.

2002. To the Honours students I offer a research report topic on the fractal patterns in Zulu wire baskets. I would like to build on the work that a colleague in Mathematics has done. One student chooses the topic, and starts with a literature review. She fills page after page, talks of the Kolam patterns that Indian women draw in the dust in front of their homes, and of Celtic patterns. She describes the grammars of the layout of Ndebele villages, and of the gables of Cape Dutch homesteads. When she hands in her final report at the end of the year, she says that she could go on forever. Patterns are everywhere, in the stone on the piazza and in the trees that line the library lawns.

In the following year she develops a program for processing grammars. She calls it GRIFFIN; I see a mythical beast with shimmering colours and sharp talons.

We let the third-year students play with GRIFFIN. Colleagues tell me that the young ones seem to have a lot of fun in the lab, developing their pictures.

The students present their work on a scientific poster. A young woman with a foreign name has made a pattern I often see on cloth and calls it 'Dabhu: Swahili for diamonds'. Another explains the grammar for the layout of Ndebele villages and points out the rules needed to expand the settlement when the chief takes another wife. Some students ask me what I intend doing with the posters once I have marked them. They don't want their posters to just disappear. They would like to take them home; they never have anything to show to their parents for their year at university.

We do a course evaluation. We ask 'What did you like about the assignment?' 'The pretty, pretty pictures,' the students say. 'The fact that you can make such beautiful patterns with such simple means.'

In the meantime, the developer of GRIFFIN has written a paper about her creation. I recruit a third-year student to create some illustrative examples. I give him a grammar I had written as a PhD student, a grammar for trees with the characteristic that the number of out-branches at a notch is not a constant, but increases steadily. Such trees are rare. When he delivers the images, he sighs that he has spent most of his time on getting the trees to grow upright, instead of to one side. I try to hide a smile; I was rather fond of my windblown trees.

2004. The year starts well. The article about GRIFFIN is accepted by a journal.

I take on a new course, a postgraduate course about the parsing and translation of formal languages. When it becomes time to design the exam, I am at a loss. I would like to have questions that are outside the realm of the recommended text. I chat to a colleague: how can I transport what the students have learned into a context we haven't discussed in class? He mentions weaving, that he once posed an exam question about it. His head of department had been aghast – such a frivolous subject in such a serious course. We begin to develop ideas about recognizing patterns. The exam takes shape. One question is on automatically finding flaws in African textiles destined for the European market. I cannot help but wonder if this is just a snazzy idea or could be developed into a business opportunity.

Later in the year I travel to Sweden and stop over in Paris. In the Centre Pompidou I stumble on an exhibition of the work of Aurelie Nemours, 'Rhythm Number Colour'. The information leaflet contains two statements that would fit in any picture gallery of mine: 'My great material is solitude; and then in making the work, time... Little by little one gets so involved in the structure of things that one forgets all the rest and nature disappears. That is the beginning of abstraction.'

> I try to remember why I thought it would be worthwhile to undergo cancer treatment. I cannot.

JANE CASTLE

# IF I HAD MARRIED A FARMER...

JANE CASTLE

If I had married a farmer when I was sixteen, I
would never have come to South Africa, and never
worked at Wits. I would never have completed
a PhD, or written scholarly journal articles, or
supervised students. I would have spent my time
outdoors, managing horses, cows and sheep. I
would have driven a tractor more than a car. I
would have worn Wellington boots. I would have
gone to Florida for the winter.

If I had married a farmer when I was sixteen,
I would have grown flowers and vegetables. I
would have planted fruit trees. I would have
made preserves. I would have cooked meat and
potatoes every day. I would have gone to church on
Sundays, to swap recipes and miseries with other
farmers' wives.

I would have had children. I would have kept
chickens and rabbits for them, and made
patchwork quilts. I would have carried them in a
papoose. I would have taught them to swim and
ride, and to read the weather in the sky.

Would I grow tired and bored of my husband?
Would we sleep in a saggy brass bed? Would I turn
my face to the shabby floral wallpaper when we
had sex? Would his weathered face seem old and
grey? His hands rough? His manners coarse?

If I had married a farmer when I was sixteen,
I would never have come to South Africa, and
never have worked at Wits. I would never have
experienced the grassy sweetness of a beehive hut,
or the mystery of San rock paintings. I would not
know the extravagance of a flowering Jacaranda, or
the violence of a Highveld thunderstorm. I would
not be the woman I am today – traveller, teacher,
writer, WonderWoman.

# MENTORS AND LOVERS

MARY RORICH

I've had lots of mentors (and lovers) in my life. Some of them doubled in the roles.

The first was, I suppose, Mr Levenstein, Zygmund Levenstein, whose Russian accent was so thick you could cut it with a knife and whose memories of the past were so meshed with the fabric of the present that I sometimes felt I belonged there too; an aristocratic Russian *dyavushka* who wore velvet dresses trimmed with fur to performances of Mussorgsky's *Boris Godunov* and Tchaikovsky's *Eugene Onegin*, and who remembered when the streets of Kiev were covered in muffling straw as Minister Stolypin lay dying. The Bolsheviks and later the Nazis had deprived Mr Levenstein of his home and culture, I imagine. He never referred to it. Nor did he ever once

became imperious and majestic: Zygmund Levinstein, erstwhile prodigy and concert pianist from Kiev. He played very little, but when he did, all glory returned to the little fat sausage fingers splayed out flat on the keys, his back stiff and proud, his face suffused with a slightly superior smile. Mr Levenstein knew there was another life. He may have ended up in a smallish town in Central Africa, but he had drunk the nectar of the gods.

My father had heard about Levenstein at work and approached him to give me piano lessons when my previous teacher returned to England. The Russian was non-committal. He would see, he said; he took only serious talent and he doubted I was that. I felt ambivalent too; after all, I was used to being the best pupil

> As for boyfriends, they were also a nonsense: time-consuming time bombs of pimples and testosterone who might give careless kisses and unwanted pregnancies.

admit to being Jewish. When I fasted on Yom Kippur because I was in love with a Jewish boy, he was mocking and cynical. 'My dear, you are working to become pianist. You need your strength. This is nothing to do with God.'

Mr Levenstein worked from eight until five every weekday as an anonymous petty bureaucrat in some government office in Lusaka. But once he had returned to his beloved wife Neura behind the thick lace and musty velvet curtains that insulated his small government house and large Slavic soul from the heat of the Zambian sun, he

of the best teacher in Lusaka and all Zambia for that matter; I couldn't imagine what an ancient Russian who had no other students could do for me. At the arranged audition I played all my big powerhouse pieces and found myself praying a silent prayer that I would in fact be recognized as 'a serious talent'. When I finished, he called out peremptorily: 'Neura, bring Miss Mary tea... we are starting now with Chopin's E Minor Prelude.' A tiny piece, something I had often sight-read, but we worked on it that day and for several weeks, until he told Neura: 'She will be a concert pianist. We have a lot to do'.

I thought weekends with the Levensteins might be a little limiting for a girl who thought also about love, delectable young men, European cities and the craziness that was being a student in the sixties.

He was a slave-driver, Mr Levenstein, and quite unperturbed about reconstructing the fabric of my fifteen-year-old life. Practising was a seven-day-a-week, if possible six-hour-a-day business. Every piece of music had to be practised slowly, and memorized, so that if he called out a bar number, I would know where to pick it up; he chose my repertoire and where I could and could not play.

Nothing 'just for fun'; everything to build the technique, the sound, the appropriate repertoire. Lots of Chopin, from studies to concertos, and Bach – preludes and fugues – and Busoni transcriptions; the fare of the great nineteenth-century virtuosos from Liszt to Leshetitsky. I lived in a dream, already a concert pianist on the stages of the world, as I walked to my lessons through the Zambian afternoon heat, thick as custard, the dust from the road filling my nostrils and my nails, so that Neura was called to bring water, a bowl and a scrubbing brush.

Every now and then I felt compelled to transgress: I played little salon pieces to accompany the school fashion show, I taught myself jazz standards and picked out arrangements of Beatles numbers on the little yellow piano my mother had bought out of an unexpected bit of inheritance. Mr Levenstein forbade me to play hockey and tennis – 'You are concert pianist, not sportsman; this is a nonsense what you are asking. Leave it to the people without talent.' Neura would nod her head furiously and look at me sadly, as though I had committed a serious crime.

As for boyfriends, they were also a nonsense: time-consuming time bombs of pimples and testosterone who might give careless kisses and unwanted pregnancies.

So, when my mother objected to a long-haired hippy who was not deterred either by my mother's academic status at the Gilbert Rennie High School for Boys or by my punishing practice routine, Mr Levenstein was a willing accomplice. 'I cannot teach you when you are thinking about this nonsense who looks like Jesus Christ. Tell him to go away and cut his hair and pass his exams.' 'His' name was Ivan and he was later jailed in Zimbabwe for being part of an ANC bomb conspiracy. I held out on Mr Levenstein and my mother for two weeks. But in the end music triumphed over my furiously hurt pride and loyalty to the beautiful Ivan – I thought he was beautiful and I liked his anarchist leanings too.

Every now and then a great concert pianist would find his way to Zambia and Mr Levenstein, Neura and I would make the trip in his tiny bureaucrat's car to the Lusaka civic centre and only concert venue. There we would promenade along the enclosed verandah of the civic centre hall, each held firmly on a portly Slavic arm, Neura and I, like some aristocratic Tzarist family, awaiting some spectacle at the Bolshoi or Mariinsky Theatre. When the Polish pianist Shura Cherkassky came, the Levensteins were really excited, because only Poles and Russians could really play Chopin and Rachmaninov, the main staple of my musical

# Does Your Husband Look Younger than You do?

**You may side-step the tragedy that overtakes so many wives . . .**

Glance about among your friends. How many of the wives look older than their years . . . and tragically older than their husbands?

Unfair though it may be, the tiny lines, the trace of wrinkles, the loss of skin tone and color, matter very little in the measure of a man's attractiveness . . . but they can make a heart-breaking difference in a woman's.

Yet thousands of women over thirty have learned to stop living by the calendar. They have found a way to deny the years . . . to combine the poise of maturity with a fresher, radiantly confident younger look. Their secret lies in the daily use of a famous cream—

Dorothy Gray Cellogen Cream. And it can help you side-step the tragedy of the middle years.

**A natural way to look younger after 30**

Noted specialists have proved that estrogenic hormones applied to the skin can help women look younger. And the hormones in Cellogen Cream are natural substances, working in the most natural way in the world to counteract the effects of the gradual loss of your own beautifying hormones. They literally get under your skin . . . work from beneath to "plump up" dismaying lines and wrinkles, give skin a softer, fresher, *truly younger* look.

**Happy results reported by women everywhere.** Thousands have written gratefully to Dorothy Gray, reporting actual results of Cellogen Cream. Here is a typical comment: "After using one jar of Cellogen Cream, my skin appeared much softer and smoother, the lines were less noticeable . . . my complexion appeared much more youthful and supple."

**CELLOGEN CREAM.** Every ounce contains 10,000 International Units of natural estrogenic hormones. Smooth Cellogen Cream into your face faithfully every night, leaving on overnight when possible. Very soon you'll see results reflected in your own mirror . . . and in your husband's look of renewed interest.
$3.50 and $5.00 plus tax.

**CELLOGEN LOTION . . .** companion to Cellogen Cream, with the same active hormone ingredient. Smooth over neck, hands, elbows; use as a powder base for effective 24-hour treatment.
$5.00 plus tax.

**HORMONE HAND CREAM.** A silky vanishing cream containing both hormones and emollients . . . ideal for telltale hands. Use daily.
$2.00 plus tax.

# DOROTHY GRAY SALON

*445 Park Avenue, New York 22, New York*

Visit the Dorothy Gray Salon and let our salon experts demonstrate the famous Dorothy Gray beauty methods. Or call PLaza 5-6110 for an appointment.

diet. Cherkassky brought his own Steinway piano with him, at great cost to both nerves and pocket; he was not prepared to risk the beer-stained, badly tuned instruments of the British Empire. He played superbly, and Mr Levenstein beamed across his huge, freckled moon-face as he told me: 'You will be as good as Shura if you work hard.'

My future was a topic discussed frequently and with urgency. The Levensteins were planning to retire in England near their son Alex who lived in Maidenhead. I would study at the Royal College and spend weekends with them, when Papa Levenstein would vet my work and my practising. Even then, despite my deep transference to a concert career and fame, I thought weekends with the Levensteins might be a little limiting for a girl who thought also about love, delectable young men, European cities and the craziness that was being a student in the sixties.

It was all resolved in the end without me having to fight for my freedom. Mr Levenstein was diagnosed with cancer of the kidney and he died just weeks after I registered at the University of Cape Town. A few years later, when I was a student at Cambridge, I travelled down to Maidenhead to see Neura. She clung to me like a long-lost daughter, tried hard to take over her husband's role, and made it clear that she planned to play an important part in my life. But a single weekend in an overheated, overstuffed English flat was enough for me. As callous as only the young can be, I never contacted her again. I suppose she's been dead many years.

# HOUSE OF READING

JANE CASTLE

Our house in Elm Street, and all subsequent
houses, was always full of books and magazines,
and from an early age I learned from watching
my parents that reading was a way of relaxing
and retreating from the world. My father would
come home from work at six o'clock every
evening, and pour a glass of whisky to drink
while he read the newspaper before dinner. He
always sat in a particular chair, and crackled the
newspaper pages as he unfolded and refolded
them. The smoke from his cigarette would swirl
above the paper, and the ice in his whisky glass
would tinkle as he took a drink. Sometimes, as a
special concession, Anne and I were allowed to sit
on his lap while he read and smoked and drank.
He was gruff, and we had to sit very still and not
wriggle, so he could read the paper in peace. He
had a big warm lap and his suits were made of
scratchy wool. He smelled like cigarettes, whisky,
peppermints, starched shirts and Vitalis hair oil.

But it was my mother who taught us to read, and
who made reading an exciting adventure. We
would snuggle up to her as she read stories at
bedtime. Cinderella fled the ball before midnight
in a pumpkin coach drawn by mice. Harriet, the
Little Match Girl, set the house alight. Fidgety
Phillip wouldn't sit still. The big bad wolf lay
in wait for Little Red Riding Hood. We looked
at the pictures and traced the words with our
fingers. We imagined being a princess, an ugly
sister, a wicked stepmother. We sang songs and
played tickling games. And in time, we learned to
read by ourselves, to escape into other worlds and
live other lives for the span of a book.

But it was my mother who taught us to read,
and who made reading an exciting adventure.

# THE GRANDMOTHER

MARY RORICH

It was important to be clever in my family. If you weren't, you might not be loved. My younger sister could add 'three peanuts for breakfast, three for lunch and three for supper' and get the right answer when she was just eighteen months old.

I was a year older and suspiciously silent. I remember my mother agonizing about a visit from relatives with particularly precocious young children: 'Ann sits at table and uses a knife and fork,' she told my grandmother, 'and she makes conversation with the adults.'

Ann's parents could not be allowed to think, to know, the worst. That was presumably the point of the tooth-mug of sherry that was forced down my throat just before they arrived. I don't remember whether I talked or not. Probably I was drunk.

'Don't worry about her,' said my grandmother of me. 'She's a philosopher; she'll talk when she's got something to say.' And apparently when I did start talking, it was in full sentences, perfectly formed and complex in content.

My grandmother was a woman of sharp intelligence and strong will who had been awarded the first performer's licentiate in Piano in South Africa. A woman whose greatest creative outlet was playing the piano for the silent movies in the little village of Maclear in the Transkei. Every Saturday morning, a brown paper bag next to her from which she swigged gin, sherry, brandy, whatever she could get, my grandmother pounded out the roulades of notes composed to evoke cowboy chases or runaway slaves or trains chugging through the western prairies. In my mind's eye she sits amidst pungent cigarette swirls, swaying slightly out of drunkenness, and smiling gently at the banality of it all.

The drink killed her in the end. But I think that another kind of death got her much sooner, a death equally inescapable. It chipped at her strong zest for life, her commitment to hours of practising; it mocked her eccentric preference for flowers and music over husbands and children. It confined her to a tiny life in a tiny town; it denied her the world she had prepared herself for, the world of pianists and concerts and

measuring herself against the best. She died of frustration and anger and hopelessness, I think, shouting to her daughters and granddaughters that it hadn't been fair for her and it wouldn't be fair for them.

But that is not the only grandmother I knew. There was the woman who sat rocking in her chair, looking out at the velvet Transkeian nights; who took me on her knee and pointed out the stars; who collected the silver paper from a thousand cigarette boxes to make

time in the Transkeian milky way, above a people unliberated and unknowing, moving inexorably towards the cruelest time in the history of colonialism and apartheid.

My grandmother died when I was six. My mother was jealous of our relationship. I talked about her often and she assumed huge proportions in my mind as a mentor for the things I wrote and for the music that was already my greatest passion. As I was falling asleep one night when I was about twelve,

## It was important to be clever in my family. If you weren't, you might not be loved.

silver balls as big as moons. And who counted with me, a little further each time: 'Ninety-nine... a hundred, a hundred-and-one...' These were moments of exquisite, towering achievement; moments when I knew profoundly the capacity of the mind as an expanding structural thing, that needed only a guide and a system to touch the world, and think and understand it. 'A hundred-and-two', and her smile crinkled round unsightly moles, facial hairs and double chins. 'A hundred-and-three' as she gently lifted me from her lap to go to the piano and play our favourite Chopin Nocturne, the one to which the stars danced in triple

Mom came into the darkened room and, standing close to my head, she whispered: 'She was an alcoholic, that woman you loved so much. We were the ones who had to live with her, apologize for her, suffer because of her.'

That night my grandmother's face, with its beloved moles and the thick coarse hairs growing out of them, appeared to me in a grotesque vision, red with purple veins, sucked up flat against the glass of my bedroom window, and cackling hysterically. 'Yes, I was an alcoholic... one-hundred-and-three, one-hundred-and-four...'

# THE SPIRIT OF OUR GRANDMOTHERS

MOYRA KEANE

She was called 'the dragon': a name that made the petite
Victorian lady's eyes twinkle. When she was seventeen she had
gone off to Burma from India to study nursing. By herself on
a river boat, then overland – in flowing long dresses and sun
hat to protect the hopelessly fair skin. How her family had
disapproved – and that was just the beginning.

...and that was just the beginning.

NORMA M. NONGAUZA-TSOTSI

# INITIATION: COMING OF AGE AND THE MOTHER'S PRIDE

NORMA M. NONGAUZA-TSOTSI

A shrill voice suddenly cried out
*Hala la Hala la Hala la Hala la*[1]

The voice pierced through the din of bubbling three-legged pots full of meat,
through the bustling and laughter of women
through the clanking of huge enamel dishes.
A woman bent down at 90 degrees, one hand warding off smoke from her face,
the other fanning the open fire with a piece of cardboard.
A ragged, dusty girl scurried with her plastic bucket to fetch water from the
zinc water tank.
'Baleka iyatsha le mbiza!'[2] the woman shouted at her.
The smell of freshly slaughtered meat wafted in the air.

Through the yelping of a dog as the old man struck it with a sjambok, adding,
'Voetsek! Le nja ifuna ukuba lenyama[3]';
Through the buzzing of green flies as they milled around the carcasses of the
slaughtered sheep;
Through slurping of lips with satisfaction and belching after a gulp of
umqombothi[4].

Raunchy and flirtatious tunes emanated from the women, anticipating a new
generation of men in the tribe.
There would be more men for the women in the village.
You were one of them.
The women gyrated and swung their hips, thrusting them forward, backwards,
as if making love to unseen forces.

*Hala la Hala la Hala la Hala la*
The voices rose – 'They are coming nabo[5]'.
The women shot out of the huts to witness.
Bubbling pots, greedy dogs and burning fires were left unguarded.
The women ululated in earnest, big hips swaying from side to side.
This was the noise of expectation; this was the victory of our customs,
through the smell of dung.

---

1. Congratulatory shouts of joy, especially by women
2. Run, this pot is burning!
3. Go away! This dog wants to eat this meat.
4. Xhosa beer
5. There, there they are

I craned my head, I pushed through the crowd.
The lyrics of the songs around me were meaningless now.
All I could hear was *Hala la Hala la Hala la Hala la*.
I turned my head and looked where all eyes were focussed.
There were voices all around, clapping and ululating with great abandon.

As the crowd stomped the ground, dust swirled around me
as if competing with the dancers.
Dust in my eyes, I squinted.
In the distance, between that dry land yakwa Luthuli e-Tsomo[6],
I could see two dots.
I sensed that the dot on the right belonged to me.
The dots became figures side-by-side, slowly climbing a hillock;
the figures became humans.

## Something stirred in me below my belly button

The unison of your steps as the two of you climbed that hillock
will stay with me forever.
Something stirred in me below my belly button
– Inimba yavuka –
the stirring of a woman who has children or who has given birth before.
My eyes were fixed on you:
floods of tears began to roll down my face.

You had the aura of newness all around you.
The long, freshly-cut white and brown stick held steadfastly in your right hand
like a shepherd;
the new black hat, that stamped your authority, placed firmly on your clean-
shaven head;
the new khaki shirt, trousers, jacket, shoes and name.

### Your faces looked down slightly, like shy bridegrooms

Your gait had changed; you seemed to walk tall with assurance.
Your steps were measured, deliberate and slow as you went down the hillock
towards the crowd.
Your faces looked down slightly, like shy bridegrooms.

I looked at you with my soul's eye.
There was that newness of spirit.

---

6. Of Luthuli village in Tsomo District

I sensed your spirit had been raised to another level:
these are the secrets that you will never share with me.
'I have acquired my new freedom: I have the right to explore,' you seemed to say.
Voices of transition echoed in my mind.
'Freedom, exploration, independence come with responsibility,' I warned.
'I know, Mom, I am ready for it,' replied the new man.

# I have aquired my new freedom

Thus stopped the spirit of conversation, with your assured and impatient response.

Left, right – pause. Left, right – pause. Left, right – pause.
Did you notice how the young boys, girls and women went into musical rapture
and dancing each time you paused, ready to take the next deliberate step?
Their expectations were palpable.
Young boys screeching imperfectly in song, hoping perhaps to receive your
blanket - evela kubhuti[7].
Curious girls flirtatiously dancing, hoping to glimpse
the new man I-Krwala[8] and would-be husband.
Elderly women and men welcoming new blood to direct the affairs of the
homestead.
*Hala la Hala la Hala la Hala la*
shouted the voices of joyful expectation.

# With every split second of a pause, pride swelled in my chest

Left, right – pause. Left, right – pause. Left, right – pause.
With every split second of a pause, pride swelled in my chest.
As you walked in that parched vastness, I could not help but conjure scenes of yore,
when African men rightfully possessed vast tracts of lands and stock.
I was seeing an African man walking alone, tall with pride of owning.
From time to time the man would look left and right; stop, turn and look at the
vastness of his wealth.
Sometimes the pause was to inhale the sweet-smelling scent of his wealth;
Sometimes to light up the long Xhosa pipe;
Sometimes to examine the crops individually;
Sometimes to examine why the cow or sheep were limping;
Sometimes to spit out long, thick black sticky mucus from his lungs.
All the movements unhurried and deliberate.
Nothing can be done without pausing and looking in all directions deliberately.

---

7. Like a new graduate, big brother
8. A circumcised man

# What secrets were you sharing?

How can you think in a frenzy?
One of you must have whispered something, because you both broke into
restrained smiles as you climbed another hillock in perfect unison.
What secrets were you sharing?
Were you amazed at the wisdom of your elders?
Were the smiles to steel yourselves against the new world you were entering,
a world that contained no formula for your existence?
Or were you thinking of how you would share your adventures with your
varsity friends?

# Singing and dancing to the sound of African drums

Suddenly, and just for a moment, came memories of the day you were plucked
from my womb,
of men and women singing and dancing to the sound of African drums,
dressed in animal skins such as our ancestors wore in the olden days.
I too was dancing.
A man snatched you, clasping your fragile left hand.
The faster he whirled you around in the circle of dancing bodies, the more you
let out that newborn cry.
Oh, the sound of African drums mingled with a lusty cry of a newborn –
it was sheer ecstasy.
I woke up from that drug-induced state, positive that your ancestors rejoiced at
your birth and welcomed you.

# As if anticipating the effervescence of my emotion

You approached.
I felt like rushing to hug and kiss you, but I knew better.
As if anticipating the effervescence of my emotion,
you slightly raised your bowed-down head,
stole a knowing glance at me,
the shortest, warmest look I've ever had,
a glance that said, 'I am a man now.'
Quickly you cast your eyes down again,
but I will never forget that look or that scene.
*Hala la Hala la Hala la Hala la*

Hala la Hala la Hala la Hala la Hala la Hala la Hala la Hala

Hala la Hala la Hala la Hala la

# Hala la Hala la Hala

Hala la Hala la Hala la Hala la Hala la Hala la Hala la Hala la Hala la Hala la Hala la Hala la Ha

Hala la Hala la Hala la Hala la Hala

Hala la Hala la Hala la Hala

Hala la Hala la Hala la Hala la

# JULIA'S WOMEN

MARY RORICH

Julia Netshivambe is a student who applied to study music at Wits in 2005 but, because she did not get any financial aid, was unable to take up the position offered her. She did a very good singing audition for her place and had already got a matric with enough points to secure her university entrance. Students are required to write a few paragraphs about their families, backgrounds and career aspirations in the audition forms for music. Julia wrote: 'I live in Mpumalanga with my great-grandmother, my grandmother, my mother, my aunts and my sister. We all live on my grandmother's pension. My mother, aunts and sister are all out of work... I dream of an education and of being able to earn a living and being able to sing...'.

# THE PEARL INSIDE

MOYRA KEANE

When I was seventeen and it was confirmed
that I was pregnant I wandered around
the streets of Jo'burg fearing to go home.
Eventually I took the last bus home and she
met me at the door with a hug and a small
silver box. Inside was a simple pearl pendant.
Mothers can do that.

# THE SISTERHOOD

MARGARET ORR

## "These are our three girls... and this is our masterpiece!"

**1965**

Three little girls, dressed identically in home-made dresses. Mine was yellow, Kathy's blue, Wendy's pink. We got new Christmas dresses every year, sewn by my mother in those days when mommies didn't work. They were always made from an identical pattern, with colour variation being the sole concession to individuality. The pastel-shaded Orr sisters – also known, fondly, by my father's congregation members as 'The Orchids'. Hearing it 'Orr kids' for many years, I could never quite 'get' why the label tickled them so. But it was a pretty mythology, and there was a not unselfconscious pleasure in being part of a 'set' of matched pieces, different yet clearly made from the same recipe, attractive, clever, cute. And we were a frivolous, feminine team – our beribboned pigtails bobbing above the dark mahogany of the front pew, as we shared hymnbooks and invented rude lyrics to old carols, trying to provoke each other into unseemly snorts and splutters of mirth. After Sunday morning service, we would stand in a sweet floral line next to the long black robes of our father, solemnly shaking hands with the exiting Presbyterians. And afterwards, in the car going home, we would snigger over the alarmingly ginger beetle brows of the Church treasurer, exchange horror stories about the damp kisses and prickly chins of the matriarchs of the women's association, or get limp and helpless with panty-dampening

fits of laughter at the moderator's hysteria-inducing tartan suspenders.

But inevitably, also, the three sisters growing up together waged an ongoing, subterranean war, fiercely contesting the identity spaces parceled out in a family. The Good One. The Clever One. The Prettiest. The Oldest. The Baby. The Favourite. Once a role was assigned, it was pretty much yours for life, however poorly it fitted, and however hard you auditioned for another one, or tried to upstage a sister who held the role you really coveted. Sisterhood meant an intense competition for limited resources – the roles allocated, the coveted colour for the Christmas dress, the fame and glory in the family (who won the Maths Olympiad and how did that stack up against being a Rag Princess?). And along with the competition went the *schadenfreude* when a sister was in trouble, because that meant you could curl up and bask in the circle of approval while your unfortunate sibling cowered in the darkness of parental disfavour.

And then the son arrived. An accident, we later deduce, given that four children must have been an unwelcome burden on a minister's salary, and remembering my mother's strained happiness in announcing her pregnancy to us. Our parents asked us to pray for a brother. I used visits to the loo to do so – it seemed logical then, as this

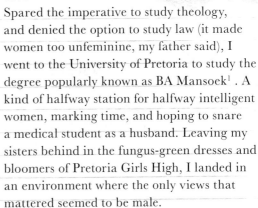

was a rare quiet time in a household full of siblings and visitors, and the only space which – albeit temporarily – was private. The cold seat of the toilet against my bottom, my feet dangling a few inches off the floor, the echoing tiles around me, I would gabble off a ritual sentence 'Please God, let Mommy's baby be a boy. Amen.' And, hooray, it was. At last my father could stop making the tired joke that he lived with a harem, in a household where 'even the dog is a bitch'. Was Chris an 'Orchid' too? He certainly got to dress in clothes that broke the pastel clone mould. Now the Orchids as a sister-act were replaced by a new billing: to visitors the four of us were introduced with 'These are our three girls... and this is our masterpiece!' Collectively, it seemed, the sisters had a new role – false starts? Inferior first drafts? Practice attempts?

I felt his arrival particularly strongly. I had been allocated the role of Father's Favourite, and as years went by without an heir, my father had resigned himself to making the best with the material he had, and I was invited into his carpentry workshop, and learnt to hammer nails, use a screwdriver, wire a plug. But then I was supplanted, before I ever got old enough

### 1973

Spared the imperative to study theology, and denied the option to study law (it made women too unfeminine, my father said), I went to the University of Pretoria to study the degree popularly known as BA Mansoek[1] . A kind of halfway station for halfway intelligent women, marking time, and hoping to snare a medical student as a husband. Leaving my sisters behind in the fungus-green dresses and bloomers of Pretoria Girls High, I landed in an environment where the only views that mattered seemed to be male.

The women students seemed silly, weak, powerless; the main aspiration of most of them (myself included) being participation in Rag Princess and *Lentenooientjie*[2] cattle calls; flirting and smiling and tossing our seventies Farrah-Fawcett locks and applying emollient to the egos of the professors (99% male), the members of the SRC (100% male), the medical students (mostly male), and – if you were truly desperate – the theological students (well, yes). Men's opinions mattered. Women didn't have opinions or power. The two dykey old bats in the department of English hardly seemed to count. Prof G was the unimaginably ancient age of 62, and had

> BA Mansoek[1]. A kind of halfway station for halfway intelligent women, marking time, and hoping to snare a medical student as a husband.

to learn how to use an electric drill. There was some relief, however, in that the expectation that I would enter the ministry was also transferred to the son, who then had to pay the price of deeply disappointing my father when he became an agnostic and studied law.

about as much sexuality or power as a knitted tea cosy, while Ms D (a mere lecturer still at age 56, shame) lectured on DH Lawrence dictating verbatim from her mouldy notes, patched together with yellowing sticky tape. She even read the punctuation marks

1. Literally – husband hunting
2. Spring maiden

The Clever One, The Oldest, The Prettiest.

('Lawrence's preoccupation with the phallus comma controversial as it was for his time comma accords with his literary subversion of the cultural norms and mores of his society fullstop.'). The incongruous juxtaposition of her humid subject matter with her dusty complexion, boy-cut salt-and-pepper hair, and notoriously inferior position in the pecking order of the English department, made her a risible and pathetic figure – not someone whom a fresh and perky Rag Princess finalist would want to emulate.

But where was the sisterhood? I looked for it in my fellow nymphettes. Twenty of us cooped up in a 'holding pen' waiting to be interviewed by the Rag Committee. Rapunzel-like drifts of hair, billowing evening gowns, a soupy fog of perfume, lips

for me, this time). It had, I am mortified to remember now, many exuberant flounces, made of white organza, printed with tiny ladybirds and – almost invisibly – the repeated phrase 'don't bug me'. It was my single, subliminal gesture of rebellion against the process.

Oh no, wait, there was another. The event – for some bizarre reason, given that Tukkies prohibited smoking for women on campus – was being sponsored by Vogue cigarettes. The flower arrangements were spiked with satin-tipped cigarettes, and artistically opened boxes of cigarettes lay on the glass coffee tables. I was a smoker and had adopted a ladies pipe which tasted disgusting but was a very satisfying finger in the face of the policy which proclaimed 'Dames mag nie

## Women didn't have opinions or power.

dripping with Juicy Fruit lipgloss. We posture and pace through the long evening hours that the interviews last, eyeing up the competition. There is a depressed flurry among the blondes at the sight of Anneline Kriel, later Miss World. She was clearly the frontrunner for Rag Queen, but there were still the four princess thrones to aspire to. (What was she studying? Do I remember? Did I even ask? It was irrelevant.) The brunettes knew they were at a serious disadvantage anyway – their one hope was to be the token darkie on the float and they stepped up their vivacity and charm, and adjusted their necklines just a little lower to out-sparkle the others. I was depressed. How had I got there? It seemed an intensely shaming event to be part of. I wore a red dress that my mother had made (only

sigarette op kampus rook nie'[3]. The policy notwithstanding, many of the women in the room were smokers too, but none of us dared to light up one of the temptingly displayed cigarettes. I think we suspected they were a trap set by the Rag Committee to weed out those candidates unsuitable to represent the flower of academic womanhood. As the evening wore on, and I suffered the curse of having a surname way down in the alphabet, I got reckless and fed up and ostentatiously began to make inroads on the free cigarette supply. Over the course of the next few hours, one after another of the nubile maidens drew me outside behind the shrubbery, frantically dragged on my cigarette, sprayed their mouths vigorously with breath-freshener, reapplied their lipgloss, and returned to the

3. Ladies may not smoke cigarettes on campus.

room to smirk and whisper behind their hands that the 'Engelse nooientjie'[4] clearly stood no chance. As a sisterhood, this was clearly not going to sustain me. It was a relief to discover, halfway through my second year, that I had

French Resistance spies in a convoluted epic that went on for days, with ever-increasing inter-textualities and plot twists) it does not really matter whose idea it originally was. It has been marvelously elaborated and

> We did not know then that in every group of WonderWomen there will be histories of abuse, of rape, of damage, of survival through immense pain and emotional mutilation.

a brain that would serve me well, and that I could drop the 'mansoek' major in my BA and do English and Psychology instead.

## 2001

The Orr kids are grown up now, and the siblings inevitably hotly contest various family narratives and memories. And we do not even always agree on who *was* the favourite. Two of us work together at a university and find professional, collegial sisterhood somewhat bemusing, as do our colleagues. The act is now called 'The Orr Sisters' and – briefly, notoriously – 'The Cabalista Sistas', and we get each other's e-mails and telephone calls and have learnt to busk answers to queries from confused colleagues about each other's fields of expertise. And together we create a New Sisterhood – the WonderWomen.

## 2002

We are at a WonderWoman retreat, the first in a series. The Orr sisters dreamed it up together – although, in the way of family narratives, we cannot quite agree on whose idea it first was. But no matter. Like the games we devised as children (playing

developed, with delighted freakish additions and complexity. Later, one of us (the 'Famous One') will sell the idea to donors, and we will find ourselves with millions of rand to spend on a grown-up game made real.

Fifteen academic women, this first WonderWoman year, trust us with their time, their careers, their stories, their flight paths through academe.

We spend five days writing, talking, training, laughing. We learn assertiveness skills. We try out Tai Chi and yoga. We form writers' groups and share our texts. We spend an embarrassed day lying on the floor with our eyes closed, incense wafting over us and New Age music playing, trying to awaken our inner womanly power. This last workshop is the first inkling we have that we are breaking into new territory in our Wits lives. It's a terrible workshop. The facilitators are young, idealistic, naïve. They hand us each a stalk of lavender; they make us lie on the floor on pieces of paper and we draw around each other's shapes with fat wax crayons. They ask us to close our eyes and recall ourselves as little girls. We are guided through memories

---

4. English girl

of unselfconscious girlhood; growing into puberty; our first awarenesses of ourselves as sexual beings, as women; our loss of uncomplicated joy and assurance. With these memories, for some of us, there is a flood of sadness and vulnerability.

We did not know then that in every group of WonderWomen there will be histories of abuse, of rape, of damage, of survival through immense pain and emotional mutilation. One participant walks out. Two start crying. The facilitators are disconcerted and out of their depth. They ask us to sing along with 'I'm Every Woman' and indulge in a group hug. Two women huddle in the

of degrees and research publications enormous. And in lying on the floor, and drawing with crayons, and lapsing into unacademic tears, we have forged a new sisterhood.

We never repeated the 'Awakening Wonder' workshop. But we sustained a commitment to 'whole personhood' as an ideal of the programme, and to sisterhood as a guiding value. One of the strong features of the WonderWoman programme thus becomes the idealistic, passionate creation of a space for support and connection. This is not 'networking'. That is what the guys do – professors pissing in each other's pockets at Senate, building 'strategic alliances',

## This is not 'networking'... This is sisterhood.

loo comforting each other. Three form a flustered, distressed group on the porch. One retires to her room, to be seen again only the next day. Some are angry. They lash out at the Orr sisters, calling us irresponsible, messing around with volatile, unnecessary evisceration. Some ask what on earth this kind of crap has to do with professional career development.

Exhausted, we pull the group together and try to debrief. It has been an extended retreat – five days. A long time for fifteen academics and the two sisters to be cut adrift from the routines of teaching, meetings, childcare, domestic duties, academic documentation and scholarly discourse. In that time, the old established patterns are shaken, the roles shift, the skins are shed – and as I look around the seminar room I am struck with a terrible tenderness for the women there. The collective IQ in the room must be staggering; the weight

caucusing, creating bridges by shared interests in soccer, cricket, rugby. This is sisterhood. A support and affirmation group, recognizing what each of us is good at; boosting flagging self-esteem; offering a listening ear when a marriage falls apart, a baby isn't sleeping, a male colleague acts like a jerk, you're having hot flushes, and you still need to teach and do research and finish that damn PhD.

In addition to the 'touchy-feely warm fuzzies', we focus on sharing hard information. As a marginalized, disenfranchised group; women on campus – we decide – need information. We need to know what is happening at the university, how it works, and who makes it work. We set as one of the goals for the programme the sharing and pooling of the high-status resource of insider information. Knowledge is power, after all. In business, they say, what matters is not what you know, but who you know. In an academic

AS A MARGINALIZED, DISENFRANCHISED GROUP,
# WOMEN ON CAMPUS
— WE DECIDE —
## NEED INFORMATION.

environment, it certainly helps to be on first name terms with Deans and DVCs, but the game is largely played by what you know. Most obviously, we have to have pieces of paper that show that we know an awful lot about solid state physics, or geological covetable and potent. It leaks – of course it does – but it tends to leak only to the insiders and the membrane is not permeable for those of us on the outside. And for as long as you do not have access to insider knowledge, you will remain on the outside – baffled and

> And for as long as you do not have access to insider knowledge, you will remain on the outside – baffled and bewildered by the opacity of the rules of the game. What you know, gives you power.

formations, or binomial theorems. But information is an even harder currency than that. What you know about the planned restructuring, about who is tipped for a plum position, about what strategic projects are being mooted, about what salaries other colleagues are being paid, about what the selection committee really said, about which research projects are getting funding... this kind of information can be critical for your survival, and also serves as a status marker.

And then there is what you know that is not really work critical, but that gives you a stash of currency in the academic board game – which two high-level university employees are having an affair, who accused whom of racism or corruption, who is increasingly indulging in fits of unprofessional petulance, what the Dean said to the DVC in an unguarded inebriated moment at a senior executive team retreat, why the VC really left, and what really happened to the lost millions in the budget. The fact that Wits – like all other universities – has strict rules around confidentiality and disclosure only makes the information that much more

bewildered by the opacity of the rules of the game. What you know, gives you power.

And so the WonderWomen pool knowledge as a core sisterly value, and – it must be admitted – as a deeply transgressive act. Mundanely, it is knowledge about criteria for promotion, and how selection committees work. It is information about the assassin's routes through the bureaucratic red tape at the university. It is passing on newsflashes about research funding available, about a special issue of a journal that might be interested in publishing what you're working on. It's information about online shopping; colic remedies for babies; the toothpaste that is guaranteed to take the taste of semen out of your mouth; how to smoke a cigar, play pool, drink wine. It's indulging in what's called 'sharing insider information' when men do it, and 'indiscreet skindering'[5] when women do.

2003
As the WonderWoman programme feeds cohorts of alumnae back into the system, there is a growing sense of a sisterhood at Wits. One participant says: 'It was like Wits

---

5. gossiping

was this dark plain, and now I can look out from my office and know that there is a glowing light... there, in the School of Social Sciences, and... there, a bright spark in the Engineering building... little dots of light all over the campus.' An increasing number of women, linked by a year of shared experience; a group of sisters to call when you need information, support, someone to read your writing to, or an ear to vent into.

And then one WonderWoman applied for a job. And I happened to know what salary had been offered an outside candidate for the post. In a burst of sisterly solidarity, I e-mailed her. 'Listen, dear,' I said, 'the salary attached to this was X hundred thousand rand. If you take the job, make sure you don't undersell yourself.' Of course, she had been offered less. A fairly standard move in the academic game, one that has led to

information. I was in trouble – cast into stern patriarchal disfavour. I had broken a cardinal rule of the Wits game, and my naïve and girlish confidences exposed as unprofessional, inappropriate, disciplinable. My source was later encouraged to leave Wits, with this 'unprofessional' transgression one of the strikes against him.

I remembered – how could I have forgotten? – delightedly running to tell a parent about a sister's transgressions ('Mo-om! Wendy spat her medicine out as soon as you left the ro-oom!') and watching with malicious delight and more than a tinge of shame as the wrath descended. But I was OK. I was the 'Good One'. Well, that time at least. But here, now, at Wits, in the eyes of the Vice Chancellor (the super patriarch), I was the 'Bad One'. And how does one recover from that in a family as Borgia-like as Wits, where

The sisterhood is flawed and frail,
and the power games are easily as vicious as
those that men play.

marked discrepancies in the salaries of male and female academics at Wits (as at other institutions), where women have not been taught to bargain or assert their value, but are socialized still to be grateful that they have work at all.

Armed with the information and – perhaps – the negotiation skills and assertiveness offered by the WonderWoman programme, she went to the Vice Chancellor. A triumph for sisterhood? But I had forgotten the ambiguities and jostlings and hidden complexities of sisterly interactions. Pushed against the wall, she revealed the exact salary figure, and the exact source of her

power games are played out in Senate, on the eleventh floor, in the Council Chamber, in the corridors and tea rooms? Well, you can resort to well-learned juvenile sibling tactics: Get her back.

At a workshop, many months later, my sister WonderWoman loses it, weeps, storms out of the debate after a messy altercation with a DVC. I sympathized, I bled for her, I worried about the obvious strain she was under. But did I keep that delicious piece of news to myself? Hell, no. And so while maybe I was still the Bad One, at least she was tainted too.
2005

Sisterhood (like 'empowerment programmes') is easy to over-sentimentalize. But sisters are too close to each other for sentimentality. The struggles for space, the absence of barriers mean that sisters see too much, show too much, share too much, to suffer any illusions. sniping hidden behind smiles and hugs and slushy Hallmark cards. We all occasionally take Lady Macbeth's advice to 'look like the innocent flower, but be the serpent under it'. Can the sisterhood exist at a university community, if not as an individual reality in

> We all occasionally take Lady Macbeth's advice to 'look like the innocent flower, but be the serpent under it'.

And the hard-nosed academic in me has read about the Queen Bee syndrome, about the research showing that women in power are more likely than men to exhibit bullying behaviour, most particularly towards their female subordinates. The navel-gazer in me knows, too, that I am susceptible to the game, and can use the survival tactics learned to cope with it, and that I sometimes find myself doing and thinking and saying things to and about other women that deeply shame me. How do I reconcile this with my passionate belief in the inherent goodness of people, and in the overriding 'niceness' of women?

From believing that only men's opinions mattered, and that the male model of the world was the only right one, I moved to a long period of thinking men were contemptible and that *gyna sapiens* was the future of humankind. Neither belief has served me well. The sisterhood is flawed and frail, and the power games are easily as vicious as those that men play. There is an inevitable admixture of love and hate in the bond between blood sisters, and this must extend to the broader sisterhood of academic women. To deny this is naïve and idealistic. To give in to it is embedding patterns of mistrust and jockeying, of nurtured and well-watered hurts and resentments, of

personal cases? One of the WonderWomen in my writer's group, listening to this as 'work in progress' suggests that what sisters often have to do is forgive the unforgivable, and move on, together. It is an act of incredible faith, to see the game, to know it, even to play it sometimes, but to trust to a fierce and sincere bond that has women journeying together.

POSTSCRIPT

I have had three children. I breastfed them all, exclusively, for the first six months of their lives. And I remember looking at my first daughter fat and chortling and reaching out to the world, and thinking: 'I made that. Me, alone. With my body, my blood, my milk. I made that.' And it was a feeling of humble power and pride. And that is what I feel about the WonderWoman programme and the sisterhood it is aimed at creating. Like my six-month-old daughter, it is snotty and smelly and leaky, and I often have puke on my shoulders. But it is a special thing, a wonderful creation, and full of a life of its own. And it has – like my daughter – made me older, made me more of the person I want to be when I grow up. I am – I think – a better sister, a better academic, a better woman. Not yet 'The Masterpiece', but maybe, at least, a more polished draft.

# ACADEMIC ASPIRATIONS
## ~ a dice game for women ~

77

78 — Cry in a meeting BACK

79

80 — Promoted to Associate Prof. MOVE AHEAD

81 82 83 84

85 — Get an NRF rating FORWARD

86

76

75

74 — Have a baby BACK to start

73 72

71 — Leave a meeting to go to the school play BACK!

70 69 68

67 — Get seconded to a restructuring project THROW a 6 to leave

66

36 — Get involved in counselling students MISS 2 turns

37 38 39 40

41 — Promoted to senior lecturer ADVANCE to 69

42 43 44

45 — Get your ADVANCE to 6?

35

34

33 — Get dumped with the big first-year course BACK to 3

32 31 30 29 28 27

START HERE — Can you make it to the top of the IVORY TOWER?

1 — Get a job as a LECTURER

2 3

4 — Take a tutor track post LEAVE the game!

5

6 — Have a baby. BACK to 3

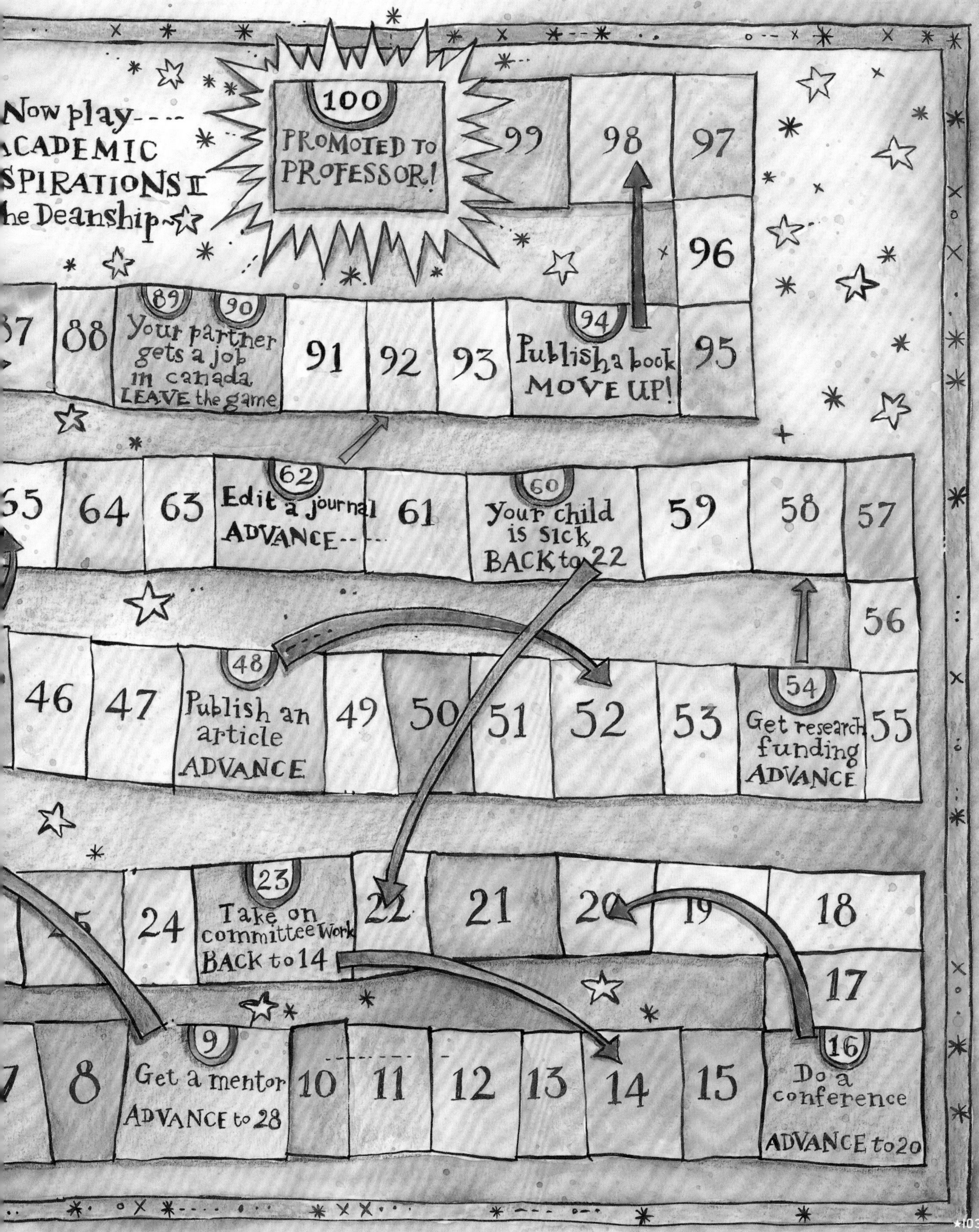

Now play----
ACADEMIC
ASPIRATIONS II
~the Deanship~

100 PROMOTED TO PROFESSOR!

99 98 97 96

87 88

89 90 Your partner gets a job in canada. LEAVE the game

91 92 93

94 Publish a book MOVE UP!

95

65 64 63

62 Edit a journal ADVANCE---

61

60 Your child is sick BACK to 22

59 58 57

46 47

48 Publish an article ADVANCE

49 50 51 52 53

54 Get research funding ADVANCE

55

56

25 24

23 Take on committee work BACK to 14

22 21 20 19 18

17

7 8

9 Get a mentor ADVANCE to 28

10 11 12 13 14 15

16 Do a conference ADVANCE to 20

*103

BRENDA KEEN

# THE WITS GAME

BRENDA KEEN

Now I work for 'Wits', and I wonder who
he is. An impossible but well-meaning ogre
perhaps? He is constantly designing new
rules, new procedures, in order to make
things more efficient. Like one of those
computer games, with ascending levels of
difficulty, and an ever-increasing list of
arcane objects to permit entry to higher
levels. The elaborate, ever-more-complex
system that the ogre designs will satisfy
everyone, meet all needs.

If you pick up the silver chalice in level two,
you can proceed through the triple-barred
doors of level three – onwards and upwards,
to dizzying heights of achievement. (A
cheque is generated in your name, perhaps?)
Of course, do not omit to feed the three-
headed dragon in level four. You would then
be doomed to wander through the abysmal
cement cool of Senate House Basement
lecture theatres.

When every eventuality has been catered
for and documented, the ogre's system will
have achieved perfection, and 'Wits' will shut
down completely, mission accomplished.

# GUIDELINES FOR CHAIRING A MEETING AT WITS

SUSAN CHEMALY

1. Arrive late. Explain that you 'forgot'. Alternatively, say that you were 'on the telephone'.

2. Ask if everybody has read the minutes of the last meeting. Ignore the chorus of complaints that nobody has received the minutes.

3. Start off by saying that there is nothing important under 'Information'. Spend twenty minutes hunting for assorted bits of paper and reading several irrelevant items. Omit the deadline for applications to the Faculty Research Committee.

4. Move on to 'Matters Arising'. Thoroughly rehash the decision that was made two meetings previously and come to the opposite conclusion. When somebody says that s/he has already implemented the decision, point out that s/he has acted without authorization and must undo whatever was done.

5. Complain at great length about unauthorised telephone bills. Refuse to take any action against offenders.

6. Complain at great length about unauthorised use of photocopier. Refuse to take any action against offenders.

7. Complain about people who hold whispered conversations, read research articles, mark test papers, eat bananas and fall asleep during meetings.

8. Be sarcastic about timid suggestions by new, young and junior staff members.

9. Be obsequious towards the high, mighty and powerful.

10. Dispense a few gratuitous insults disguised as 'humour'.

11. If any important matter dares to raise its head, squash it immediately.

12. Conclude the meeting. Notice that both secretaries are absent and that nobody has taken any minutes.

CENTRAL BLOCK

# SELECTION PANEL

BRENDA KEEN

Seven months pregnant, slowing down,
my body engaged at two levels – creating new life,
and surviving this one.

I get into the lift on the eleventh floor, push the button. Before the doors have completely closed, howls erupt from my throat. I press my head against the wall of the lift, knuckles into my mouth. As we pause for a pick up on the ninth floor, I hide my tears behind a curtain of hair, keep my head down.

I stride along the concourse, groping for my cell phone. I dial the number of my friend who is looking after my baby. She is on the campus, but I cannot wait to speak to her in person. The baby will be hungry, and I still have to race to school to pick up the small boy.

The phone connects, and I howl. 'Oh God, it was so horrible, I want to die, I just want to die.' As I exit Central Block I see a lecturer unlocking his office door with his head down. I never even talk to people about suicide, but for now I don't care that he can hear. I just howl. I feel unemployable; I don't feel fit to live.

The incoherent sound alerts a member of Campus Control, who calls after me: 'Miss, Miss, are you OK?' I turn, gesticulate wildly, keep on walking. I'm very late. On the other end of the phone, my friend is telling me to 'breathe, breathe'. And she tells me to stop and look over the library lawns, to calm down a little, not to upset the baby.

The interview was for a promotion that I didn't really want. I had come back from holiday to be told that my position had become redundant. Because of the reorganization of workloads, I would have to apply for a more senior position, and hope to get it, or be retrenched. Seven months pregnant, slowing down, my body engaged at two levels – creating new life, and surviving this one.

Now it is five months later, and I have been for the alternative promotion interview, just in case. I had thought I knew what to expect: nine people around the table in the council committee room. 'Where do you see yourself in five years?', 'What are your strengths and weaknesses?' When I had told my son that I was going for an interview he asked if I would be on television. 'No', I laughed, 'Just a bunch of people, sitting around a table, asking questions'.

I did not anticipate that the questions would be loaded. I forgot that when there is an internal candidate we structure the questions around every foible, every flaw, every fault that we can find. Internal candidates have preference over external – in theory. In practice, the panel knows exactly where to stick the knife.

Yes, I did not finish everything before I went on maternity leave. I got tired, after six months of overtime, and then the redundancy issue. Not to mention the terrible week's holiday, the mugging on the beach.
No, I did not carry out the final checking of

the brought forward balances; I just made sure the closing balances were fine. I did not reallocate all the individual balances. Later I will remember that I was not on the committee for that task. My job was to publish the global figures on time, and this I did.

No, I did not finish everything before I went on maternity leave. Every year the auditors say: 'There is a risk here, that only one person knows how to do this'. But in the interview I splutter and stammer, and forget that I am just an ordinary human being, doing the best I can. No, I did not finish everything.

They question my accuracy, and shake their heads. 'What do you do, if you have made

My answer describing my management style is not sufficient. They ask, by name, about a staff member who seemed to have a problem with me, some years ago. What would she say about my management style? I skirt the issue. 'Personality clash' sounds so vague. I could never ascertain exactly what the problem was. Too much work, too little recognition? It doesn't seem appropriate to discuss someone else's issues here, amongst strangers, in this room where my mouth has become so dry.

What is my greatest professional achievement to date? I can think of nothing, I am like an animal slowing down, as the predator moves in for the final strike. Passing the Board exam at the first attempt seems so long ago.

## I had put some journals through the wrong way around, and then corrected them. I expect I should go out onto the Great Hall steps and disembowel myself, to atone.

a mistake?' I said 'You fix it, try not to do it again'. This answer is not enough. The professor looks at me over his spectacles. How can you be an accountant if you are not accurate? He shakes his head and turns away.

Accuracy. The auditing profession typically uses a 'schedule of unadjusted differences'. Here it is several pages long, with other people's errors and omissions. I report on what the general ledger says – with no automated computer system or human help. Just me, and six lonely months of pregnancy, lugging the laptop between home and work. I had put some journals through the wrong way around, and then corrected them. I expect I should go out onto the Great Hall steps and disembowel myself, to atone.

Everything else seems so lame. Was any of it ever any good? I'm limping along to the homeward stretch.

And then the final horror: there are points on my references that they must quiz me about. My body wants to get up, lumber out of the room. But I stay. 'You are inaccurate, you are not committed, you are not emotionally strong enough for this post.' I want to say: 'Yes, there are elements of truth in all of those', but I'm not ready to write myself off completely. What is commitment? To what? To whom? I worked all that overtime, this year and last. What does that mean? Their faces show that it means nothing, nothing at all. And emotionally? Yes, I do take things very hard.

At other people's interviews I have listened to those carefully worded enquiries about doubts raised by referees. They're meant to give the incumbents a chance to defend themselves. In reality, though, that incumbent is dead on arrival. And now I know how painful it is.

I doubt whether the panel members know anything about narrative framing. Someone else – Tin Man, from The Wizard of Oz, for instance – would have picked up different issues, formed a different opinion. This same

I drive home, drink three glasses of wine, take some painkillers, and fall into bed. The baby and I sleep. At three in the morning I sit at the top of the stairs. I have not cried so much since all my diligent, middle-class illusions died. My heart is so swollen in my chest that I can no longer feel.

It's been years since the thought of committing suicide drifted around my head – I hoped that I had finally outrun the pain. But after the interview I find that my mind conjures up an

## And a quiet night-time place, where I won't be rescued by some well-meaning arsehole.

referee had said, in June, that I had a good chance of getting this job. (But perhaps a better chance of jumping out of the window and missing the sharp stones below.)

I cannot wait to leave the interview room. I smile like a dead person. Yes, I am quite sure that I will be hearing from the HR person next week. She has been quietly sitting here all along, writing down the questions and answers, not noticing that blood is being shed. I've observed before that she often seems to be doing the mental equivalent of filing her nails.

I stagger away like a maniac. The lift comes, to contain my pain, and to carry me away.

I see my friend and I allow my emotions full expression. I feed my baby and try not to sob. I phone and reschedule things, so that I don't have to race across town immediately.

My friend says 'You know who you are', but I don't, I just don't. I thought I was a competent and hardworking employee, but I'm not. I howl. I don't know who I am.

image, and returns to it, over and over. I see myself driving into the night in my white car. I felt so proud and grown-up when I bought it – my first 'real' car. That was two years ago, when there were different elements in the narrative frame: I'd had a large salary increase, was happy working here.

Now I am 38, picturing the smoke-filled car. All it takes is a hose, some rags and some tape. And a quiet night-time place, where I won't be rescued by some well-meaning arsehole.

As I was preparing to write this piece...

LEAH GILBERT

# LOST (AND FOUND) IN TRANSLATION: 27 YEARS AT WITS

LEAH GILBERT

As I was preparing to write this piece, my eyes were distracted by the daily paper lying on the table. As usual, I headed straight for the horoscopes (me of rational and logical thinking – this is my daily indulgence). Alas, no miracles for me today:

*Leo: Some of your ambitions and projects should be shelved until a more favourable session comes around. Anticipate delays and setbacks; yet curb your impatience and be prepared to wait it out because your fortunes will improve once again. ('William Smith's Stars', The Star, 7 April 2005)*

Not a promising start to a day intended to be devoted to the writing of my piece for the WonderWoman Book of the Century.

Don't we always have to curb our impatience and be prepared to wait? To make sure that your fortunes will improve, isn't it about putting in the effort and producing the goods?

I began to think about what constitutes a 'successful academic' or 'good academia'. We often use these terms as fixed measures against which to make important judgements about people's career paths – and ultimately their lives – and they are goals towards which we are all, presumably, striving. But aren't these notions dynamic and constantly shifting?

Surely there is no singular definition: these objectives imply different things to different people at different points in time. In short,

## What does the taste of success mean, anyway?

My mind moves slowly; it is still early in the day, so I try to distract myself with my surroundings...

*Things may not always go according to your desires during the forthcoming 12 months yet you must not cave in, in any instance. Make a habit of having spare plans and alternative arrangements as safeguards. Then you will taste success. ('William Smith's Stars', The Star, 7 April 2005)*

Regrettably – or perhaps fortunately – I did not read these instructions at the beginning of my academic career some 30 years ago. I wonder: Would things have turned out differently had I had such advice, or taken such 'instructions' seriously? What does the taste of success mean, anyway? Aren't delays and setbacks part and parcel of any career?

these are contested concepts – because they are socially constructed concepts – and they should be treated as such. A changing social context would undoubtedly mean changing conceptions and priorities, and correspondingly modified evaluation criteria. And, more often than not, these changes would be accompanied by shifts in power bases relative to the new criteria for evaluation. A reflection on my own academic development helps to illustrate this argument.

As a child born in Poland three years after the end of the Second World War to parents who survived the Holocaust by a timely escape from Warsaw Ghetto, I was acutely aware that I was brought into this world with great expectations and hopes for a 'new and better world', as my mother used to say, 'a world without wars and

> Like most of my friends and second generation Holocaust survivors, I was a memorial candle who had to shine for all to see how we've survived.

hatred'. I guess, after emerging from such a nightmare my parents genuinely believed that 'it will never happen again' since the 'world has learnt a lesson' – after all, this is why they decided to have another child to replace all the lost ones. Like most of my friends and second generation Holocaust survivors, I was a memorial candle who had to shine for all to see how we've survived.

Israel was fighting its War of Independence and was established as a Jewish state, and anti-Semitism was raising its head once again, so we left Poland to go 'home' – a place we'd never been to and whose language we did not speak. With the vision of a better future we landed in a new country struggling for its survival. Ironically, as a child born to celebrate peace, I found myself as a young soldier in the Six Day War (1967), had my wedding on the first day of the Yom Kippur War (1973) and, having married a South African who wanted to go 'home', arrived in Johannesburg on the eve of the June 16th riots.

In between the wars, I graduated with a degree in Sociology, Statistics and Computer Science. I went on to complete a Masters of Public Health so that I could combine my theoretical knowledge with the practical experience I had gained in the army and later in the *Magen David Adom* (Israeli Red Cross) as an instructor of medics and first aid personnel.
I arrived at Wits in 1978. This was the year of the famous Alma-Ata[1] declaration promising 'health for all by the year 2000'. My thinking at the time was profoundly shaped by this new approach, as was my teaching philosophy regarding the role of medical sociology in promoting Primary Health Care in South African medical education. Whenever I broached the topic of incorporating this approach into our teaching programme for health science students, however, my senior colleagues responded with blank faces. First, they responded with polite dismissiveness: 'Are you sure you are not translating it incorrectly from Hebrew?' This later turned to disapproval and censure, as they did not consider it relevant or important. They were probably wondering: 'How can we allow this young foreigner whose English is not that great to challenge the way we think?'

Needless to say, this state of affairs did little to advance my career or improve my fortunes. I did not feel good about it, but had no time to dwell on it; my mother always used to say, 'make the most of any circumstance', and I tried to do just that. I was working part-time, had two babies to look after, and was content in the knowledge that I was keeping up with the latest literature, and giving my students the best I could (regrettably without the endorsement of those responsible for the advancement of my career – those with the power to improve my fortunes). I was convinced that I was practising good academia based on cutting-edge research and developments in the profession, but

---

1. The WHO conference in Alma-Ata, Ukraine was where the concept of Primary Health Care was fully developed, and it established the global cornerstones in Public Health for years to come.

at that stage there was little congruence between my convictions and those of the powers-that-be. 'She is isolating herself and doing her own thing,' they criticized, while I was developing an innovative programme tailored to the needs of the dental profession. 'She's never here – what is she doing?' they said in private (and sometimes in public), while I was working with a multi-disciplinary team on comprehensive health promotion programmes at schools in Riverlea and Soweto, or contributing to the training of primary health care nurses in Tinswalo Hospital near the Wits Rural Facility. But this was the early 1980s, when these were not considered valuable academic activities in my department and Faculty.

I continued, committed to my ideas. 'You must have had a really thick skin,' a sympathetic colleague says years later. No doubt the thick skin, combined with my mother's survival kit, was of great help. I knew that I had completed what was at the

health centre, but they could not stop the ideas; these left South Africa together with the academics and flourished elsewhere, at the same time denying many communities appropriate Primary Health Care for decades to come. According to the criteria of the time these academics were not engaging in good academia, although many went on to become pioneers of innovative public health programmes in Israel, the United States, and Australia[2].

While apartheid policy made sure that progressive ideas such as Primary Health Care remained hidden from public view for as long as possible, I was increasingly fired up by new developments and structured my teaching around them. 'As future health professionals you have a social responsibility', I would tell my students. 'It is not just about your knowledge and skills: the people's needs and where they are coming from are as important. Appropriate medicine can only be practised when health and illness

## 'But how can you deliver the babies if there is no electricity?'

time one of the most progressive courses in Public Health. Ironically, the ideas for my course were originally conceived and developed in the Polela Health Centre, Valley of a Thousand Hills, Natal, in the 1940s, physically only a seven-hour drive from Wits but academically years apart. Polela's originators were prohibited from practising their kind of progressive Primary Care in South Africa because the political authorities did not consider it important to 'improve the health of the Bantu'. They closed the

are understood in the social context of the community'. But who is 'the community'? Most of my students at that time did not come from the communities to which I was trying to sensitise them. Following the guidelines of good pedagogy, I tried to expose them to some of those communities. We organized trips to rural hospitals and clinics in Hammanskraal, and to urban centres such as Soweto and Alexandra. We would visit health centres, speak to the people there and then (with their permission) go to

2. For more see: Gilbert L. 1995, Sociology and the "New Public Health" in South Africa. South African Journal of Sociology, 26: 1-10

The committee, composed mostly of white males, has
officially approved my professorial status.
I am legitimate. I must have done something right.

# Or am I dreaming?

their homes and try to imagine their lives with no running water and no electricity. 'But how can you deliver the babies if there is no electricity?' asked a student in Hammanskraal. 'Oh!' replied the nurse in charge of this ill-equipped clinic, 'it is difficult, but we manage'. Of course, babies were born before there was electricity in the world – but was this appropriate in South Africa in the 1980s?

The students could see all this; I could sense that they were thinking, they were feeling; and they were learning things relevant to their career, at least as I understood it. Back in the classroom they told me that they loved it, they wanted to read more and do more visits. Some students told me that it now made sense to them to study Sociology. And I loved it too; I learned along with them. They went home and wrote reports; some even wrote poems about the newly-discovered world of 'diverse communities' in South Africa and their un-met health care needs. And I went back to colleagues who tried to discredit me. 'She is not really teaching Sociology,' they argued.

Unbeknown to me then, what I was doing was to develop into what is now widely recognized as community-based education using a multidisciplinary approach, which is encouraged and emphasized wherever possible. In 2005, this is good academia!

While I was doing my innovative interdisciplinary bridging, however, I also managed to slip between the cracks – no recognition, no promotion, not even a tenured position; just a temporary contract renewed every year for 12 years. All I had

were my convictions, my students' feedback, and my loving Jewish mother's wise advice: 'Why are you so worried? So you'll be a professor a year later!'

'How did you manage to bear it all?' asked a young colleague and friend years later. Again, my mother's advice came in useful: 'Concentrate on what you have and not what you would like to have'. And, as I told my friend, I had my family to keep me going – luckily, there was lots of recognition and *naches*[3] there. And I also had my daily aerobic classes to keep me sane.

I was too busy to think about 'spare plans and alternative arrangements as safeguards' as my horoscope might have instructed. I dutifully did my best under the circumstances, as my mother had always told me – my mother, who had no formal schooling, but earned a PhD in the science of real life and survived the worst, always assuring me that 'There is nothing bad that something good does not come out of it'. As always, she was right.

The HIV/AIDS epidemic with all its devastating effects has brought with it a new awareness of the interconnectedness between health, disease, and society. It has also put the spotlight on the inadequacies of our health care system to cope with our health problems, particularly where disadvantaged communities are concerned. Thus, it has made what I've always done look more important, timely, and relevant, and perversely has contributed towards the improvement of my fortunes.

Sixteen years after my arrival at Wits: transformation in South Africa, and a new

3. joy

government concerned with its people's health and welfare. The ANC health plans echo my language and I'm beginning to feel part of a bigger project. By now I also have a 'real' job at Wits, a full tenured position as a lecturer. I'm safe and secure. I concentrate on my research and teaching; new courses follow, new research projects are initiated. Suddenly Primary Health Care is a buzz-word in professional circles. I'm playing a significant role in the now-recognized movement of the New Public Health in South Africa. I'm even part of a multidisciplinary team sponsored by the Kellogg Foundation that visits schools of Public Health in Europe and the USA, so that we can use their lessons in the establishment of a School of Public Health in the former Transvaal – a project on which we have been working since 1991.

It is now the summer of 1994; Mandela and the new democratic South Africa are dominating the headlines, and the red carpets are rolled out wherever we go: Boston and Harvard, Columbia, Chapel Hill, Ann Arbor. We listen, we talk and we are listened to, we are familiar with the language and the terminology – and we recognize that although we have been away for a long time, we are now joining the global Public Health community. And I feel great. Suddenly I'm not translating any more – my language is understood as is. It is even spoken by our colleagues in the best schools of Public Health, and (again irony raises its head) these scholars are familiar with the ideas and the South Africans who pioneered them, but who had to leave their country to pursue them.

Twenty-five years later, and I am now tasting success. I am a WonderWoman and I can do anything. Although it took me so long to become an Associate Professor, I got there. What I do, although similar to what I've always done, is now recognized by most as 'good academia'. My skills are called on too often for me to be able to respond. I sit on committees of experts, who now listen to what I have to say and don't whisper in the corridors behind my back. I am put forward for a promotion to Full Professor of Health/Medical Sociology. A phone call from the Dean, 30 minutes after the interview, confirms that the decision was unanimous: the committee, composed mostly of white males, has officially approved my professorial status. I am legitimate. I must have done something right. Or am I dreaming? I don't have the official letter yet – is it real? Perhaps my horoscope was right: my fortunes have improved once again and, true to my mother's prediction, I became a professor a year later.

The question I cannot fully answer now is whether it was worth the struggle – my gut feeling, however, is Yes, Yes, Yes!

But before I get too excited, I check today's horoscope:

*You need to display real courage in order to overcome the obstacles that are now confronting you. Be prepared to deal with annoying people and irritating conditions. ('William Smith's Stars', The Star, 4 July 2005)*

Maybe my journey is just beginning? 'The important thing', the horoscope continues, 'is to keep your wits about you in all cases.' So here it is, Wits, I am keeping you with me despite it all...

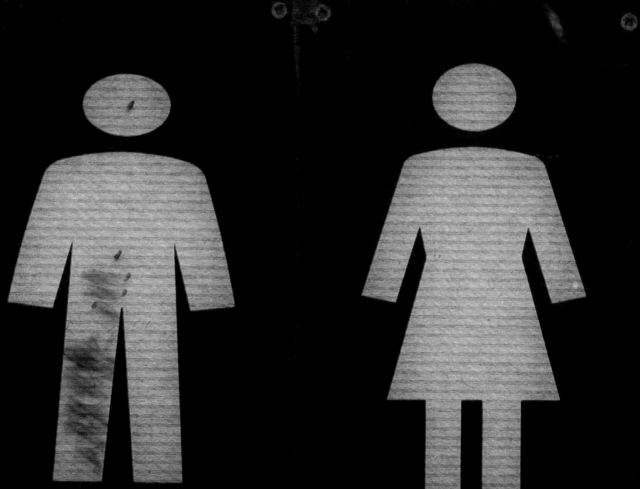

# TWO IN A BED

MOYRA KEANE

How grand it sounds to tell friends that the university is sending you to present a paper at an international conference in the USA. In un-academic fashion I wear lipstick to have my visa photograph taken and wear a smart jacket to the embassy. The conference fee and air ticket cost a little more than the Research Office has allocated. I pack muesli and dried fruit.

Four of us will share a room – with only two beds. My unknown bedfellow is a young woman from Iceland. (Found each other on the Internet!) I meet her in the hotel foyer: we laugh... 'You must be the person I'm sharing a bed with?'

The two men in the room at least know each other.

It had sounded so grand.

My talk is scheduled for the last session, last day, in a tiny room in the basement. 'Curriculum issues in Africa' is not a hot topic.

But then neither is 'Gender issues in Iceland'.

# THE DUSTY ROAD FROM CRADOCK

NORMA M NONGAUZA-TSOTSI

Though I was born in the sandy Langa location in Cape Town, the seeds of my future life were sown in Cradock – a small Karoo dorp in the Eastern Cape – between 1955 and 1961. Lwana Primary School does not physically exist now, yet it is deeply etched in my memory, and therefore lives on. 'How can that be?' you ask. Because I am telling the story and you are reading it.

The school and the surrounding locations fell victim to the grand demolition plans of the apartheid system. The reason was simple: to form a buffer zone between the white residents and the black townships.

Cradock still brings to my mind dusty roads, foul-smelling, brown, brackish water and prickly pears. However, it is a place, when I look back now, of unsung heroes and heroines

matter how outdated. We had no library facilities in the community or at school then.

Ms Nzube, Ms Rhunu: in my childish eyes, these two were not just the best teachers in arithmetic. I secretly admired them for their impeccable dress sense, neatly plaited hair and ladderless stockings. (There were no pantyhose then.)

Miss Mary Nongauza was my aunt, a high school teacher. There were always all kinds of books in her house, and she put no boundaries on what I could read. Restrictions were imposed only by my own incompetence and disinterest. No doubt she gave me this leeway in order to encourage me to read, but a hidden intention, I now suspect, was to distract me from the incessant talkativeness for which I was known. Children's books were

> Woe unto you if you got pregnant, especially if you were single. You would lose your post immediately.

in education. I breathed the same air, drank the same brackish water and walked on the same dusty roads as they did. I will name just a few, so that you the reader, if you are so curious, can find out for yourself about these people. Some have long gone from this earth; some have feeble minds now, but their children and grandchildren live on.

Mr Luphondwana was my principal. I recall him exhorting the pupils in the assembly line to read newspapers – even if they could not afford to buy them, they could pick up discarded copies in the street to read, no

everywhere in the house. I also distinctly remember my obsession with the *Reader's Digest*. I would read it from cover to cover and bombard my aunt afterwards with questions about the meaning of words, even when these were explained in the text.

When Mary left for overseas to further her studies at Oxford on a Rhodes scholarship – I think I was about eight years old then – I stayed with two extraordinary sisters. One was a nurse, Mrs Luxomo, and one a teacher, Miss Mdaka, affectionately known as Sisi Koko (the latter was buried recently near

Queenstown). She was an exquisite teacher and a narrator par excellence.

Around the fireside on Friday nights before prayers, Sisi Koko would read out loud passages from the English prescribed books that her high school-going children and nephews had as their homework. She would bring the characters of the books to life. Books which she characterized so well, and which stand out in my memory, were *The Hound of the Baskervilles*, *The Thirty-Nine Steps*, *Julius Caesar* and *Macbeth*. Those memories

that whilst one inspector was in a class where English was being taught, the others would go to an arithmetic class. The teachers would have to demonstrate their capacity to teach and the inspectors would afterwards inspect the pupils' books on their desks.

The teachers solved the problem of the book inspection by playing musical chairs. Pupils who were known to be very strong in a particular subject would be placed strategically at the end of the desks in front and at the back of the class, forming a

One's dreams can bear fruition long after one has forgotten about them, and way back then it was a pipe dream – a black African woman would never be allowed to lecture, especially in a dental school at Wits.

of a female-headed family, taking turns in reading out loud to each other around a fireside, are among the most vivid of my childhood in Cradock.

Like all the young girls at that time, some of my reading material also came from magazines like *Zonk*, *Drum* and *Bona*. If I ran short of books or magazines, I would listen to the wireless (as it was called then) – my weekly favourite story was 'Consider your Verdict'. Listening to radio talk shows is still my favorite pastime even now.

School inspectors were a regular feature in my primary school. For some reason I only remember tall, portly, white males. They were assigned according to the subjects of their expertise – arithmetic, English, Afrikaans, domestic science. Each cluster would go to different classes in the school, so

formidable flank to protect the weaker pupils who were always huddled safely in the centre. These vanguards would shoot their hands up, their tiny fingers clicking against each other, shouting 'Miss! Miss!' to catch the teacher's attention and answer questions posed by her or the inspector. Of course, their perfect books were also conveniently within the inspector's reach.

I was one of those strategically positioned in my English class (although not in arithmetic, which I dreaded). We would show off our work to the inspectors with pride, and answer all their questions in English to their astonishment. I do not know whether these inspectors eventually grew wise to our tricks. Now I think that what we did was a form of quiet subversion, part of the passive protest that was beginning to take place in black schools against Bantu education. Cradock, after all, was the home of the heroic Cradock Three (Goniwe, Calata and Mhlauli). You could not have lived there without knowing about the inequalities in South Africa, even at my age then.

For many of my generation, women nurses and teachers were our role models. African women nurses and teachers in the fifties were regarded as temporary-permanent staff. Woe unto you if you got pregnant, especially if

*not lie: though it tarry, wait for it; because it will surely come, it will not tarry.* One's dreams can bear fruition long after one has forgotten about them, and way back then it was a pipe dream – a black African woman would never be allowed to lecture, especially in a dental school at Wits.

Thus my journey into realizing my dream of an academic life began here at Wits in 1997, in my midlife, a wife already with two

## ...in an early meeting, a professor mistook me for a secretary.

you were single. You would lose your post immediately. The only thing that sustained your sanity was the respect you received from the community. You further earned respect by being a holder of a BA.

In retrospect, I believe I am not in an academic environment by coincidence. It is a choice I made many, many years ago, though it would be fulfilled much later. In 2002, four years into my present employment, going through my old papers (I am a chronic hoarder) I came across a copy of an application I had made in 1979 to an international organization, requesting financial assistance to study. One of the questions on the application form required a motivation as to why I wanted to study. The reason I had given was, 'I want to teach in a university in South Africa one day'.

This wish was fulfilled seventeen years later, when I had long forgotten about that written intention. It reminds me of the Lord's advice to Habakkuk in the Old Testament to write down his dreams – *For the vision is yet for an appointed time, but at the end it shall speak, and*

children beginning to find their own paths in this wide world. The only weapon I was armed with was a dental degree – no whisper of a higher degree (my nursing and midwifery experience did not seem to count in the same way) – and experience of working in the public sector outside and inside South Africa. This was a time of excitement in South Africa, three years after 1994. Like many people, I felt it was the right time to make a contribution in the tertiary education arena, especially to young black Africans who had been scarred by Bantu Education.

I was the first female black African dentist to be employed full time in the dental school. It was quickly confirmed (without malice I believe): in an early meeting, a professor mistook me for a secretary. This assumption did not anger me as it would have done before 1994 because I understood that African women tended to be stereotyped in a certain way. He quickly apologized when I was formally introduced.

I had been in the past a member of Medical and Dental Councils in Lesotho, Transkei

and eventually the Interim Medical and
Dental Council of South Africa. Perhaps that's
why my first assignment was to coordinate
a course on jurisprudence, ethics and
practice. A lecturer who had been around the
dental school for many years was assigned
to assist me. For some inexplicable reason,
the appointments with this lecturer never
materialized. I had no clue how the timetables
were structured as I was not a Wits alumnus.
Coordinating the course was a nightmare: it
was an attendance course and not examinable,
so not popular with students. Few students
ever attended the 7h30–8h15 classes. Those
who did were half asleep or arrived just in
time to sign the register. Not surprisingly,
they slammed the course in the lecturer
evaluations. I tasted my first and last bad
evaluation from students. The following year I
galvanized experts in the field of jurisprudence
and ethics, never again to have a course poorly
evaluated in a field that I was not prepared
for myself. Years later the course was taken
over by appropriate departments; it is now
compulsory and examinable.

**Ha, Verwoerd!**
You destroyed my dreams of Langa and Tsomo.
They say I cannot read or write in English, therefore I am stupid.
They say I cannot count, therefore I am stupid.
Now I am in dentistry, but there are no other black women.
I am a black woman, I must be the secretary.
They will give me a course to teach – that is my job.
But they will give me the worst course, the course the students hate, a course I have no
background in.
And I will fail. But only once.
I will win the Vice Chancellor's teaching award, I will do research.
But still I will not get promoted.
Ha, Verwoerd, do you think you have won?
Never!

**Whatever your shape, size and proportions...**
Berlei make a foundation to fit you perfectly
and offer you the personal services of a highly-qualified
corsetiere: the 'girl with the Berlei badge'.
You will find her in most good corsetry departments
and you can trust her judgment implicitly.

*One of the beautifully
fitting Sarong range with
patented criss-cross front.
Only Sarong lifts and braces
tummy muscles, never rides up,
gives you an exhilarating
sense of comfort and freedom.*
BERLEI SARONG 4404 77/6
SARONG BRA 400 27/6
*Brit. Patent Nos. 647114 & 755556*

*Berlei shapes you lovelier...for life!*

# A LIFE LESS AVERAGE

BRENDA KEEN

I've never been bored. I have the *Reader's Digest* to thank for this – one copy from the seventies in particular. As a child I read there that intelligent people are never bored. And I have always wanted to be intelligent.

In fact, that's why I have two handwriting styles. The fast, sloping writing was developed in response to claims by my brother and his friends that boys have sloppier handwriting than girls because of their superior intelligence. I don't think this handwriting made me any brighter, but it was useful when my mother would whizz me down to the library in her little Anglia for last-minute project work. This was before photocopiers came to Kempton Park. I would quickly scrawl the info I needed in my 'My Big Block Book'.

Cats. Lions. The mating habits of the rhinoceros. What a medieval fortress looked like. My essays always came back marked: 'Use your own words'. I puzzled over this. Eventually I figured out that they wanted me to use words of one syllable. (I had been changing the encyclopaedia's words around. My love of the passive sentence goes way back.)

So I paraphrased the World Book in monosyllables and my essay marks improved. What can I say? School was strange.

In standard three, strangers come to our school to give us intelligence tests. We sit in our yellow and brown winter uniforms, in long rows in the school hall. Short green pencils, and multiple choice booklets. Anxiety gnawing away at my stomach. My secret is about to be exposed.

I refrain from chewing on the pencil that is not mine, and try very hard to get the answers right. A drawing of cog-wheels, loads of them. What direction is 'F' turning in? I have to close my eyes and picture a clock, to work out which is clockwise, and which is anti. I look at the cogs and ponder. Do they all move in

So I paraphrased the World Book in monosyllables
and my essay marks improved.
What can I say? School was strange.

the same direction? Or opposite directions? I don't know anything about machinery. So I pick the one where they're all moving in the same direction. I turn the page with a sense of the wrongness of my answer.

There is a section containing different series of numbers. You have to work out which number comes next. I have no clue, so I just guess. Years later an engineering student will explain to me how each number corresponds with a letter of the alphabet, and that's how you work it out. That small girl with two long plaits and yellow plastic bobbles had no chance. I still don't get it, actually.

Then the section on English, which is so simple it makes my head spin. Hand is to glove as foot is to...? No, really. There must be a catch. Shoe, pathway, bridge, macaroni. My eye picks out the answer, and my brain makes no sense of it. My English teacher is at the front of the hall, wearing high red mules, and pulling her jersey closer against the cold. There is no help there. We close our books, hand them in. I walk out feeling completely numb. My days as the high achiever princess will soon be over. Every teacher will know my secret shame.

I had been doing well at school until then, but I knew the tests would reveal that I had been faking it. I'm not clever, but I work hard. The loss is huge. Being clever, doing well at school – these were all I had.

I remember how pleased I was at the small amount of recognition I got once for being able to spell 'audible'. Mrs Robbins – of the frivolous shoes and sensible cardies – had predicted that no one would get all the answers right. But I did. She asked me how I knew how to spell it, and I shrugged, as

pleased as pink. Did I know what it meant? Eyes down I shook my head: not so much inaudible as just plain speechless. I was blazing inside from all that visibility.

We never did learn whether we passed or failed the intelligence tests. After a while I felt that each teacher looked at me with a kind of pity. I slunk past the unasked questions in their eyes. How did you fool us for so long? The word 'average' burned in my heart.

Years later I was at work at the 'Big D' supermarket when we heard our Matric results were out. We all piled into Mrs Cowie's mustard-coloured Toyota and drove down to the school. I collected my one page from the office and burst into tears upon opening it. Mrs Cowie put her arms around me and comforted me. But she was mystified when she saw the result. One A and six Bs. I didn't get a distinction for my beloved English. And inside my head, a leaden word throbbed.

Average. Average. My secret, hidden shame.

Now it is nearly two decades later.

I've qualified in my chosen profession and studied English for fun. I got my BA with a distinction in Psychology, though. That's the subject that saved my life.

I've been in therapy for a decade and a half and learned how to be seen.

I've supported a family and a doom-laden enterprise that never got off the ground. I adopted a child, bracing myself against the possibility that he had HIV. Eventually his mother's antibodies cleared out of his system, and the future opened up again.

I ended a marriage, survived a custody battle and a psychologist's 32-page report which burned new and painful scars onto my heart.

I found my true home, in a valley in the Eastern Cape. One day I hope to return. In the meantime I survive, here, in the world that is not mine. I broke my own heart, and

pieced it back together again.

I saved the life of a woman with HIV. It was simple, really. I could not let her go. It was Christmastime, and the doctors were away. I drove in and out of Orange Farm in the small blue Uno; fetching her, taking her back. Her CD count was 29, but within six months she was back at work. Now she says to me 'till death us do part', and I know that she travelled much further than me, on those trips.

I had a baby this year. Now I have my own small family of three. My adopted eight-year-old son was given room for all his feelings: the aching loss that he felt, never having known his real mother, the feelings of displacement. He is doing well, and shows affection toward his new sister. I am secretly proud that he has the vocabulary of a ten-year-old. I am secretly proud that I am a good mother.

Now there is no time to worry about measuring intelligence, and no place in my heart for the word 'average'.

My secret, hidden shame.

SIGRID EWERT

# REDS, GREENS, SOME YELLOW

SIGRID EWERT

A sunny room.
Yellow walls, recently painted.
Pictures of big red flowers on the wall.
Poppies.
I have always loved poppies.

A comfortable chair.
A needle in my hand.
The nurses are busy, efficient in their movement.
They are cheerful and polite.
They say all the right things.
They must have done a workshop on modern medical practice,
and listened well.

The minutes pass.
The bag with saline solution is removed.
I flex my hand.
A new bag gets attached.
CMF.
A poison by any name is just a poison.

I settle back, try to make my hand limp.
It should hurt less that way.
I read my travel guide.
*Let's Go Spain and Portugal 1998.*
I am going.
They just have to remove the needle from my hand.
That's all.

In the chair next to mine is a middle-aged black man.
He doesn't read, he just sits.
Perhaps he cannot read.

A nurse goes to him.
'I'm sorry', she says, 'the treatment is damaging your kidneys.
We have to stop.'
They remove the needle.
He thanks her quietly.

I want to hug him.
You don't hug strange men.

He gets up and walks out of the room.

With my free hand I page through a stack of magazines on my lap.
They present the fashion for the coming winter,
also the latest hairstyles.

There is hair on my pillow every morning.
There is hair around my feet in the shower,
swirling around the drain,
often clinging to a foot.

In my frantic attempts to rub it off with the other foot,
I sometimes lose my balance.

I must be more careful.
Bruises, cuts and burns won't heal easily.
They could get infected.

Recently I ran into my landlady.
'I thought you lose all your hair when you do chemotherapy,'
she chirped,
'but yours is so beautiful.'
Since the diagnosis three weeks ago I've become an expert on these matters.
'No,' I say with authority, 'no, you don't necessarily lose all your hair.
It depends on the chemical they use, and the individual.'
The counselling nurse had offered me the loan of a wig,
adding that they had only blonde ones left.
That had caused some mirth in my family.
My youngest sister, who since birth has been as white as milk,
welcomed me to my new life as a dumb blonde and stated that
we now finally had more in common than specialist knowledge of computers.

A nurse comes to check the needle.
'Do you have children?' she asks.
'No,' I reply, 'none.'
She tells me that there is an inverse relation between the number of children a woman bears
and the probability that she'll get breast cancer.

I could tell her that she shouldn't believe everything the head of the oncology unit says,
even if he is a German scientist as you see them in luxury car advertisements.

I could tell her that I am also a scientist,
that my friend is a medical researcher and has
provided me with articles from prestigious journals on this matter.

I could tell her that she is speaking from prejudice, not fact,
that cancer is not punishment for not conforming.

I don't bother.

If I had known that my brother would be diagnosed with a hormone-related
cancer within eighteen months,
I would have had more belief in my facts.

A large dark-skinned woman gets up.
She has radiant skin, glossy, slightly wavy hair.
I noticed her dress this morning already.
I like it; it is very colourful, reds and greens, splatterings of yellow.
When I complimented her on it, she gave a broad smile.
Her front teeth are missing.

With my complexion I could never wear a dress like that.
I would look ill.

She announces proudly that the treatment of the past months has shrunk her
tumours sufficiently to make surgery possible.
She adds that she is going shopping.
She cannot go home.
If she did, there would be trouble.
Her husband doesn't like her leaving the house.

A nurse stops at my chair.
She has seen in my file that I am at university.
Her daughter would like to study medicine next year.
Could I give her some information?

I want to tell her that I didn't sleep last night,
that I dread the long journey home in the blinding summer sun.
My eyes have become so sensitive,
my skin curls up at the slightest suggestion of sunlight.
I want to tell her that I don't even want to think,
let alone talk.

Statistics go through my mind.

In the West, one out of four gets cancer.
In South Africa, one out of eight women gets breast cancer.
No-one carries the letter C.
I tell her what I know.

In the corner of the room there is a bed.
I could ask to be moved there.
The energy required to change from a lying to a standing position
is more than that from a sitting position.
I stay where I am.

In the chair opposite mine there is now a young boy,
approximately ten years old.

Red hair.
He doesn't look scared.
He doesn't look anything.

He has a big box of toys on his lap, some clearly brand new.
No care-giver.

He clutches the box and stares ahead of him.
I catch his eye, I smile.
I'd like to make him laugh.
I pull faces at him.

He doesn't respond.

# SYLVIA MUNSAMY[1] - APRIL 6, 2005

MARY RORICH

Sallow-faced and anxious; furrows of self-deprecation above the jet-black eyes. 'Indian', I thought, taking in the red bindi on her forehead. And yet the wild halo of dark hair was African: frizzy and shoulder-length, with a broad grey streak forking like lightning from a jagged middle parting. Smiling a nervous apology in advance, she sat down at the piano. 'Should I play?' and her hands fumbled through one of those clappy-happy, second-rate hymn tunes. Her singing voice was little and quavering, a sing-song translation of speech incubated in the coloured suburbs of apartheid South Africa.

'How will she ever cope with the brash self-confidence and virile talent of students less than half her age?' I wondered. And will she be able to jolt an out-of-practice mind into the 'poly-hetero' jargon of the postmodern?

for 2005. I discovered she was of Khoisan extraction, by the way, and that her husband was Indian and a small-time entrepreneur. She had three children, all of them at Wits.

I thought about and saw Sylvia Munsamy often. She would squeeze herself against a wall as I walked past, or take several steps back when I approached her. She would stammer out a 'Good morning, Professor', her voice choked with awe – and joy. Her face was like a flower, I thought, a flower slowly turning towards the blinding, wonderful sun, a growing sunflower breathing in brightness and transforming and becoming glorious. A sunflower saying, 'At last I understand what it is to be in the light; how blinding, how brilliant, how glorious it is.' I saw her shining out of the middle of packed lecture theatres. I saw her beaming at Bach; at a visiting

## 'Well, these are the things that happen to women who want too much'

Never mind. Give her a chance. Suggest she watches the movie *Educating Rita*. No don't. Rita has just got her daughter to accept her as a co-university student when she discovers she's got Alzheimer's.

And so I signed Sylvia Munsamy into the Foundation course of the Bachelor of Music degree. I thought she'd probably get cold feet and withdraw, any way. I thought her husband would try to dissuade her. But she didn't, he didn't. Sylvia Munsamy turned up in February as an official B Mus student

cellist, at marimba jives and drum riffs; at little African songs and flashy opera arias; at sonatas and symphonies. I saw her sitting amongst fellow-students, laughing quietly with them, enjoying their boisterous, bragging bonding. I saw her bent over music staves, her wild bright orb of hair painted into a moment of concentration and ecstatic intensity.

I checked her marks yesterday. Rows of eighties and nineties signify in yellow highlighter that she will be fast-tracked to the full first-year music course in June.

---

1. Names have been changed.

'But where was she for last week's test?' the Music Theory lecturer asked me. 'She never misses a class.'

I knew. She had come to me in the morning, her sunflower face turned sallow again, and twisted into a pleading, desperate agony, even while she apologized for bothering me. Her husband had had an attack, she said... behind the wheel of his car. The tests were all negative but the doctor had put him on medication for his heart and blood pressure. He might have more attacks; there might be something terrible, something the doctor hadn't found. He worked too hard, she said. Sunday to Sunday, 'even on Christmas and New Year'.

'Sheer stress?' I asked. 'Perhaps he needs to take it easier.'

'Yes', she replied; 'he's very stressed. He's only 52. But he won't stop; he's a one-man business, working for his family – imports imitation jewellery from India. There's no one to take over. He's a good man; he treats

married and earning: if you don't have to look after your grandchildren, that is.'

But her eyes were pleading, begging me to find a solution. And in that moment I knew that I was a woman even before I was an academic. I had to take on this fight as much as if it were a young black student desperate for education and money. What had we women of the sixties and seventies fought for, if not to make it possible for those women less lucky than us to have lives beyond child-bearing and home care?

I had fought tooth and nail to keep a career as a married woman; had refused to simply give up my job at Wits and follow my husband to Cape Town, even though my family and friends tried tactfully to tell me it was my duty, and that I had a good, loving and very patient husband. I demanded marriage counselling, went into therapy, argued furiously about my rights, about my contribution to a new South Africa. I threw a lamp-stand at him one night when he

## An impossible, selfish woman.

his staff so well... they think he's stupid; they take advantage of him. The family all think I should take over the business; I can feel their eyes on me. I feel so selfish. How can I be thinking of myself at a time like this?'

I felt completely blank. What could I say? What did she want me to say? 'Well, these are the things that happen to women who want too much'; or 'You don't have any choice: surely you love your husband?'; or 'You can come back when you're a widow, when you are no longer a wife; when your children are

said I didn't earn enough for my career to count; and broke down the bedroom door at the Mount Nelson Hotel on a weekend surveillance trip to Cape Town. He'd locked me and my impossible feminist demands out, and I felt like a child, unheard, bereft, inconsolable.

Most people would say that I lost my marriage in the process of negotiating my feminist identity; and I sometimes wonder myself if the cancer that killed him just a few years later had not been caused by the strain of an increasingly complicated, dysfunctional marriage. An impossible, selfish woman.

Ten years later, I still have weeks of darkness and turmoil, nights when I sleep a furious sleep of sorrow and disbelief, and wake to a colourless numbness of soul and psyche that leaves me lethargic and without hope. The blame goes round in my head, the wishing it had all been different. Wishing I could do it over; could make the right choice. Wishing I had had the stern authority of love and intimacy in those last years that would have allowed me to say: 'I have made an appointment with a dermatologist and you are going to have that mole on your cheek looked at.' I commented on it, of course, worried about it; but no longer had the right of a lover to say: 'I couldn't bear it if you died... Please, please, do this for me.'

What does this have to do with Sylvia Munsamy? Would I wish on her remorse, the accusing stares of her children, the increasing bitterness and withdrawal of her husband watching her nurture a new love? No, of course not. But isn't it time that we women were spared the agony of making impossible choices? Were spared the burden of guilt that spells 'wife' and 'mother'?

'Guilt is not an emotion', said one of my lovers of the eighties. 'Well then, why do you play on it every time you don't get your own way?' I would like to have responded. Like the time in Los Angeles when I wanted a chocolate Brownie for lunch on New Year's Day – and a cup of instant coffee. And you said I should choose a pastrami sandwich on rye and stop reading my book. 'Narrativity is so 1970s,' you drawled from your couch across the room, your blue-veined elephant balls hanging out beneath the bottom of your Japanese dressing gown, your lower lip sagging onto your famous, brilliant jowls. And 'Why do you think South African composers are so lousy?' you challenged me. What were you trying to make me feel, if not guilt? If not guilt about the fact that you were bankrolling this awesome, glamorous trip, then guilt for not just giving in gracefully, down to the detail of a chocolate brownie. You used to introduce me to the rich and famous with 'This is my future widow'. And that did make me feel guilty. Because I had a perfectly good husband at home.

You see, Sylvia Munsamy, I was not a good wife; I wasn't a good mother either. Although I cared most of the time, and tried my very best some of the time, and was in constant dialogue with myself about why I wanted more and why it was never enough. I don't know the answer to that. But I do know that I deserved to own my mind; that my education, my passionate engagement with music and my enormous sense of having something to give generation after generation of students have been profoundly important to my growth as a woman. I could not have stayed at home and produced good meals and appropriately servile and empty conversation at dinner parties. I could not have relied for my mental stimulation on bridge – the cultural alternative offered me, although I doubt you can relate to it. I could not have confined my love of music to singing in the church choir, and playing Classic FM in the kitchen while the family watched the TV news.

I was lucky, though: I had a mother who was determined her daughters would be educated and have careers, perhaps because her own intellectual dreams were so compromised by her marriage. (Not that she would ever have taken a stand, or even consciously have wanted a different kind of life.)

I have been empowered as a woman; I have studied at the best universities; I have partly penetrated the glass ceiling. I am more or less happy with where my career is going, and I know that I will grow old with ideas and books and colleagues whose minds and conversations I enjoy.

So, Sylvia Munsamy, even if I have to bend a few university rules, I am going to make it possible for you to run the fake jewellery business on Mondays and Fridays, and attend those classes you can on the other days. I am going to tick your name on registers when you're absent and give you my own notes if you need them.

I will remind your other teachers that they are women too and that they owe you compassion and an education. I will remind them that they fought for this, for you; that an education is not only for getting a job in your twenties, it's for illuminating your world in your forties, in your fifties, even in your eighties. And I will tell them that we at Wits will fade if your sunflower face is deprived of its light.

And if your husband dies? I can't promise that you won't feel guilty; I can't promise that you won't scratch at the loose skin around the little wounds and needs that he couldn't fulfil in you, and try sometimes to wish them away. But I can promise you that this light that has come so late and so strong in your life will not go out. And that I'll be there for you as a woman and an academic.

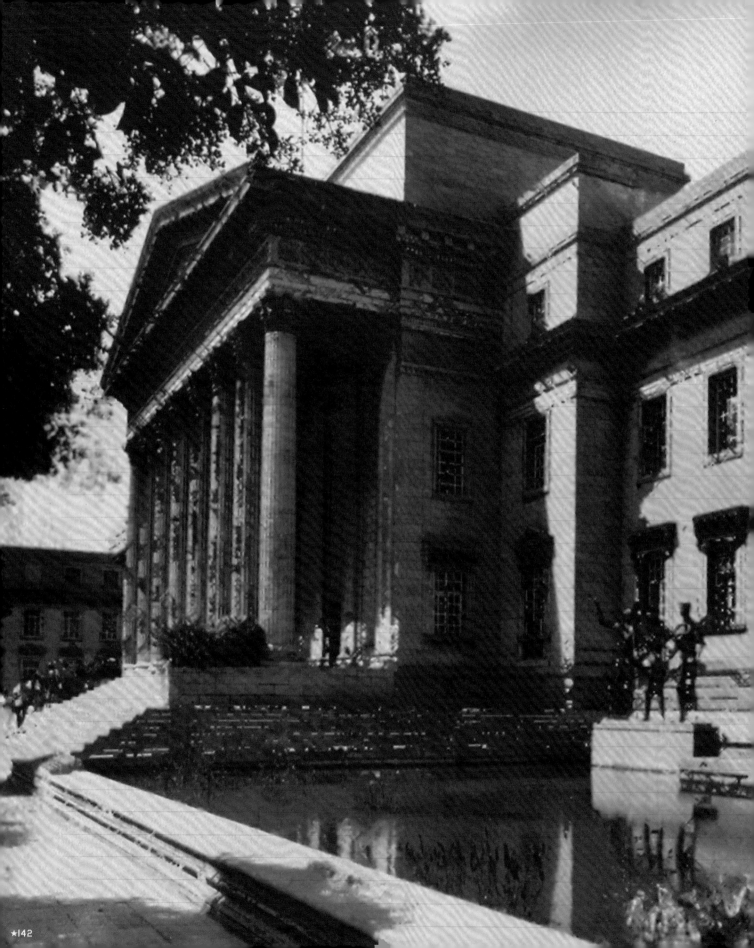

# THE FACE OF WITS I

MOYRA KEANE

The great fluted majestic columns of our public mask: proclaiming an ancient European ancestor, unchanging stability, grand masculinity but hiding countless private stories so we don't know who we are...

★143

The Wits Corporation

★144

Karen Lilje

# THE FACE OF WITS 2

BRENDA KEEN

The Face of Wits has so many facets, it's difficult to get to know him. He strides down corridors in shiny black shoes and straight-legged suit pants. The black gown flaps importantly around him. Staff and students step back, lest we impede his progress. We retreat to our offices, with our personal stories and our private pain. Sometimes we

female Buddha that my friend gave me. She watches my struggles to be a good mother, a decent human being. There is no blame on the face of the Buddha, only compassion.

As I think of Wits as a woman, a new image emerges, like a radiant bird from the slumbering Great Hall. The sky

## I think God was just too 'Faculty of Commerce, Law and Management' for me.

ponder why this institution, which prides itself on having fought injustice, should be such a painful place at which to work and study. Not all the time, of course. Of course.

These are my projections onto 'Wits', much like the projections of my young self onto God, in His mysterious three-piece suit. His Plan for Your Life. The impossibly high penalty for not accepting the 'free gift' of salvation. I struggled then to relate to God, as I struggle now to relate to 'Wits'. I think God was just too 'Faculty of Commerce, Law and Management' for me.

When my younger self started to think of God as a woman rather than a man, things fell more into place. Perhaps the 'Face of Wits', too, could be female? I think of the different faces of my fellow WonderWomen, and the administrators that I deal with daily. I think of the delicate porcelain face of the

clears, blue. A breeze blows in the chaos of possibility. Now Wits has a hundred arms, and a hundred roles, just like a woman. She holds all her children with tender care, no matter how different, needy or disdainful they are. She listens to all their voices with compassion, tries to make a place where their needs will be met. She tries to get them to play together nicely, while she makes dinner, marks papers, thinks about her research proposal.

Wits, the woman, leads the transition to inclusivity and tolerance, respect and kindness. She is vulnerable, like all women, to the risk of neglecting her own soul. We must draw this new being into the fold, nurture her. She is mother, sister, friend, colleague, co-conspirator. The face of Wits smiles enigmatically, like a Buddha. The folds of her academic gown flap around her feet, where the journey is about to begin.

# DEGRADUATION

JANE CASTLE

Recently, I've been having a recurring dream. In it, I walk up the steps to the stage in the Great Hall at Wits, wearing a black gown rather than my usual red one. I give my card to the Dean who nods solemnly. I take a deep breath and look about me. I notice the hall is packed with graduands and their parents. My friends and well-wishers, who resemble the cast of *Sex and the City*, are in the front rows. They are wearing pretty party dresses, chatting, waving, calling out to one another and to me. They are behaving inappropriately, but I am happy to see them. I walk towards the Vice Chancellor, who smiles at me genially over the hideous mace, a symbol of his authority. As we lean towards one another to shake hands, the corners of our mortarboards bump against one another. He is unscathed, but my cap goes askew, twisting my hair painfully. The mortarboard rides up on my head. It looks ridiculous, I know, but I don't care. I smile for the photographer and, in a dramatic movement, remove my cap and toss it to the crowd, as if throwing a bridal bouquet. It flies through the hall like a gigantic frisbee. The crowd roars. Women leap to catch it. It sails over their heads and lands with a thump in the dark, dusty recesses of the hall. I walk to the alumni officer and turn to face the crowd. He helps to remove my gown and hood. Cameras flash. My friends clap and cheer. Someone at the back of the hall ululates. As the gown slides down my arms, I start to fly, first awkwardly, like a turkey buzzard, flapping around the hall, then, like one of William Blake's angels, I hover blissfully above the fray.

In another dream, I am again on the stage of the Great Hall, dressed in an academic gown, but this time I am holding out a tasselled brocade cushion with a crown on it. I am giving this crown back to the Vice Chancellor and the Dean. It is too small for me, I explain respectfully, and too shiny. It does not fit. I do not want it.

But we all get here, in the end.

# RETREATING: DE HOEK, MAGALIESBURG

MARGARET ORR

We arrive in dusty, heated cars. Many of us got lost, couldn't find the way. The maps were unclear, we say. We thought we had to travel straight at the first intersection, the turn-off was so sudden, the signposts were confusing, the roads weren't labelled. One of us broke a spring on a speedbump even before she got out of her suburb; another punctured her tyre on the rocky dirt roads. One got halfway to Ventersdorp before she realized she had to turn back.

But we all get here, in the end. We straggle up the steps to the stone house, past the roses smooth as the white cotton sheets on the high four-poster beds waiting for us in our rooms, but we have harder travelling still to do. The programme tells us we will be surveying and digging, mapping the terrain, walking our writing, mining and crafting.

Early this morning I took leave of my partner. He was off to retrench 5 000 miners at a gold mine. It is unimaginable. The highway to the Free State, the dirty, noisy, towering machinery of the mine, with the dark tunnels into the earth underneath. Five thousand miners – their muscles sweating and aching

## Is this real work? Maybe not, but somehow the retreat still feels too exhausting to contemplate.

and the lavender, the warm polished quarry tiles, to a space where white flowers lean out of vases, breathing soft colour over us. We carry suitcases, laptops, briefcases leaking urgent bits of paper picked up at the office, handbags, a wide-blue-eyed baby in a papoose, the baggage of our lives. We have fended off last-minute e-mails, done an online grocery shop, left lists on the fridge about suppers, notes for the school teacher, instructions about feeding the cat. We have arrived.

The first day we are still smeared and bleared with toil. The grime of our journey and of our lives still clings to us. The Wits weariness drags our shoulders down. We may have navigated our way to this umber yellow conference room, with its gleaming wooden table, the black-covered journals at each seat, their pages as fresh and clean and

from labour I can't begin to understand – waiting with empty eyes for a letter, a small amount of cash, to join the unemployed millions in this country. I will be writing, reading, listening. Having breakfast and tea and lunch and tea again. Is this real work? Maybe not, but somehow the retreat still feels too exhausting to contemplate.

I am dry, clotted with words in stagnant pools of memos, policy documents, guidelines for 360-degree appraisal, proposals to the Senior Executive Team about academic-related job tracks. This retreat suddenly seems like a really dumb idea. I am heartsick and disillusioned about my work. I don't know where I'm going with it anymore. I have lost the sense of travelling hopefully, and am reluctant to start any journey unless I know where it is going to end. I have mislaid the compass sense I once had, the guiding North Star. In the past weeks colleagues have complained to the Vice Chancellor that equity development programmes are misguided, unnecessary. That the retreats offer inappropriately luxurious and sybaritic indulgence to selected few, while students starve and budget cuts have denuded the toilets on Wits campus of paper towels.

We talk about it in the first session, before we even start the work we must do. We talk about guilt – do we deserve this? This quiet green space, the warmth of the underfloor

awry by impatient fingers searching the scalp for the right words. Mary loses colour as the retreat goes on. She wears faded tracksuits and no lipstick. Her eyes look tired, dark-circled. Only her hair riots on in electric exuberance. But at evening readings she clothes herself with a tapestry of writing, stitched with the colours and glowing silks of sunflowers, dragonflies, and Japanese gowns. Our words make us beautiful. The writing that emerges as women read to each other is full of 'others' – of students and colleagues and mothers and grandmothers and fathers and daughters and lovers. It is an unselfish

> I feel the blood of Amazons coursing through the satisfying pull of my arm. The arrow flies sweetly, impelled by muscle and taut bowstring, and misses the target entirely.

heating in the bathroom with its huge tub and tall windows open to trees murmurous with doves? The flowers and candles at dinner, the flashing white smiles of the staff bringing us coffee in the morning? We remind ourselves how mean and pinched our lives are, how hard we work, how unaffirmed we feel at Wits. We talk about the interplay between affective environment and our inner wellsprings of creativity. We talk about needing permission to turn inwards, to write 'selfishly'. We talk about the privilege of what we have, and what we owe in return. And then we start work, uneasy still that we are rationalizing our indulgence, but determined to mine the rich seam of the next few days for all the jewels that we can find.

We write ourselves into nakedness. The make-up fades, the hair gets messier – scrunched into careless ponytails, raked

outpouring of love and observation and reflection of the family of humankind, and an intense and unblinking self-reflection. Who am I? What have I done with my life? How do I know that it is good? How did I get here? What have I learned about myself and how can I share it with others? How do I write this all in a way that offers meaning to others?

Pam and I are 'walking our writing'. I am stuck, blocked, feeling paralysing performance anxiety. I cannot do the exercises. I cannot play, flow, experiment. Brenda takes six nouns and six verbs and writes a page of story, beautifully curved, like a smile, in upon itself – neat, perfect, satisfying. I am tight, panicky. What can I do with 'orange', 'photograph' or 'memory', and 'curl' 'swing' and 'dive'? How can I write the first sentence of an eight-sentence story

when I don't know what the last sentence
is? I find myself trying to fetch the ending
before I can start the beginning. I want the
breath-catching denouement, the 'aha', the
epiphanic arrival before I've even started.
Pam and I walk in aimless circles, under
trees, next to the river, talking. We find a
small path, sodden with the first brown decay
of autumn accumulating as the trees let slip
their leaves, overarched by bright berries.
'Where does this go?' I wonder aloud, and
then splutter out a laugh at myself. I look at
Pam. A delicate wood dryad, she waits – as
she does in the workshop – with eyebrows
arched, the corners of her mouth curved, her
silence an invitation, a space for me to fill. I
answer myself: 'Well, we don't know where
it ends. But this is where it starts.' We take
the path. We find a horse – huge, muscled,
smelling of sweet grass. He huffs against my
hand, the whiskers on his pink nose tickle
my palm. Pam offers him some grass and he
takes it from her hand with huge yellow ivory
teeth. Quietly, comfortably, we walk back to
the glowing umber space of the conference
room. This afternoon we will do archery, and
that will be good, too.

We have tea and pecan pie under an open
green tent on the archery field. We clown
around, hitting hay bales and making ribald
suggestions about the black-bottomed target
of our instructor. Luckily few of us can even
figure out which our dominant eye is, so
his rear-end is safe. The wooden bow fits
satisfyingly into my hand. I feel the blood of
Amazons coursing through the satisfying pull
of my arm. The arrow flies sweetly, impelled
by muscle and taut bowstring, and misses the
target entirely. Three tries later it lands with
a richly satisfying thunk in the yellow ring,
and I am jubilant.

# NANCY DREW

JANE CASTLE

In December, I stayed in a cottage on a friend's smallholding in Kyalami while my apartment was being renovated. I would return to the cottage in the evening, grimy and exhausted from supervising students and builders, and get into a hot bath with one of the books left behind by my hosts' teenage daughters. My favourites were Nancy Drew mysteries. I read three in a week.

Why was Nancy Drew so appealing, not only to pre-teens, but to a 50-something WonderWoman? Was it simply nostalgia? A memory of reading Nancy Drew at

often and joyfully. She never travels by bus or train, and rarely flies, thus avoiding the tiresome queues and delays which ordinary travellers experience.

Nancy doesn't remember her mother, who died when Nancy was a child. The household is run by an unobtrusive housekeeper, of indeterminate age and race, who is devoted to Nancy and her father. Nancy has no domestic responsibilities, but she can always rely on a warm reception, clean clothes, and her favourite meals when she comes home. Home is a place to recover and regroup

> She is the woman we could be, if we had worthy parents, devoted partners, and reliable household help

summer camp in Georgian Bay? Or had the combination of exams and grout gummed up my brain? I decided to apply some detective skills of my own to solve this mystery.

For the uninitiated, Nancy Drew is a student at an unnamed Ivy League college in New England, who solves mysteries during her frequent vacations. It seems she doesn't have any readings and assignments to do over these breaks, nor does she have to work to pay for tuition and accommodation, so she can apply herself to detective work in her considerable spare time. Nancy is unencumbered by academic and financial responsibilities; she is mobile, too. She has a driving licence and her own car – a red roadster (or convertible in the updated editions of the books) – which she drives

from the rigours of detective work. No one reproaches Nancy for not coming home more often, or for bringing a suitcase full of dirty laundry with her.

While it is sad that Nancy grew up without a mother, there do seem to have been some compensations. There was no one to intervene in Nancy's vision or plans for herself. No one to criticize Nancy's clothes, hair, or figure, or her choice of friends and music. No household chores. No little brothers and sisters to babysit. Nancy has never told tales or lies. She has never known anguish or guilt. Nancy's role model is her father, a successful, but unobtrusive lawyer, who travels a good deal for work. He frequently takes Nancy with him, and she is always welcome in his practice. He is unfailingly polite and respectful to women in general, and always supportive of Nancy. He does not drink, smoke, watch rugby on TV, or come on to Nancy's friends.

Nancy's father doesn't tell Nancy what to do, or how to do it. Instead he asks for Nancy's help in solving puzzles and following up clues and inconsistencies. He rarely provides direction, but he is always available for advice. He is good at logistics and resourcing. He praises Nancy for her keen intelligence, her creativity, her persistence and skills of deduction. He is the perfect father.

Nancy has an enquiring mind, and she works through problems logically and deductively. Occasionally she follows a hunch, but she is not an impulsive or intuitive person. She is persistent and thorough, never diverted from her investigations for long. She is assertive and resilient. Nancy is often assisted by two girlfriends who are clearly not Nancy's intellectual or social rivals. They are easygoing companions who form a showcase for Nancy's talents.

Nancy also has a perfect boyfriend, Ned, whom she met at college. Ned is good-looking and amiable, and appears on the scene when Nancy needs physical assistance to solve her mysteries. Once he built a bridge of saplings to help Nancy cross a moat to a castle where an eccentric recluse had concealed a stolen fortune. Another time, he put out a fire in Nancy's motel room. When Ned has done his job, he goes away, leaving Nancy to get on with her work. He never demands sex in exchange for favours, or indicates that Nancy should devote more of her time and attention to him, or wear sexy lingerie.

Isn't it obvious by now? Nancy Drew is the dedicated, effective, successful and fulfilled woman we all dreamed we would become when we were ten or eleven years old. She is the woman we could be, if we had worthy parents, devoted partners, and reliable household help. She's a woman with an education, a brain, and opportunities to use them for the benefit of many. She is us, in pure, unsullied form, a WonderWoman, on a mission to change the world.

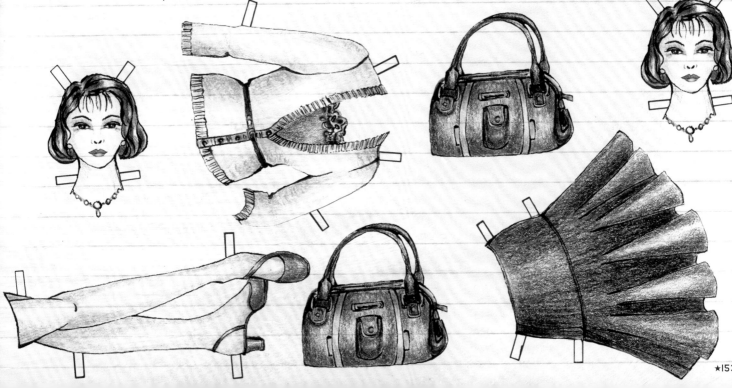

PAM NICHOLS

# VILLAGES AND PATHS

PAM NICHOLS

I recently found the first home I knew. In my mind it was a perfect place: a neat cottage covered in creeper in a country lane, bluebell woods behind and a pig farm further down. As a child I roamed with freedom there, played with a gang of children and spent from morning to night in the woods. When we moved, I was desperate to return. At age ten, I pedaled 30 miles to look at the cottage we had lost. Now in middle age, in the UK on sabbatical from Wits, I see a sign on the road and on a whim turn to see if I can find Cold Harbour Lane. It is easy to find and, to my joy, it is gorgeous. The small redbrick houses seem to have grown from the earth; there are bluebells in the woods. I am amazed that I could find my beginning so easily, that it is so unchanged and so peaceful.

That first safe home gave me the wish to explore and the belief that I could. It didn't give me a direction though, that became clear after Lebanon.

I did English at Sussex without much difficulty or event, though I was lucky enough to get to know a professor who inspired me and who has remained a friend and mentor. Sussex was notable for international men such as the Lebanese engineering student with big smiling eyes. He turned out to be from an extraordinarily rich family. Wealth brought them suspicion and unease but I loved the way the family were with each other. When the father said, 'One day you must visit Lebanon,' I nodded, and thought it impossible.

This was probably why I jumped at the chance when it came. My professor received a request for an English teacher to teach in a village mountain school. I had finished my degree and wanted to travel.

I packed a bag, with one evening dress in memory of evenings with my ex-boyfriend, and found myself looking out of the window of a Middle Eastern Airways plane. This was 1980 and I was going to a part of Lebanon that had not been involved in any recent fighting. I was going to a remote village in the Chouf Mountains to live with the Druze. The Druze religion is a schism of Shiite Islam, known fully only to the elders. The Druze believe in the transmigration of souls, which means that you cannot convert and become a Druze, you have to be born, or reborn, as one. Historically Britain has taken their side, with France championing the Christian Maronites. I knew a little of them from reading about the demanding, large and dramatic Lady Hester Stanhope, the eighteenth-century niece of William Pitt, also from Kent, who ended up in a castle in their mountains, holding séances and entertaining travellers like Kinglake. I had a print of her castle perched on a rock. I didn't exactly think of myself following her footsteps but I was aware that not many westerners had lived among the secretive Druze. I leaned forward on my seat in the plane and stared through the window like a trapeze artist about to leap out and catch the arms of another.

The sky was full of clouds that looked painted, pink and bright on one side, on the other dark. We were fast approaching Beirut and I leaned further with no idea of what I would see. We flashed through clouds. I think

The sky was full of clouds that looked painted,
pink and bright on one side, on the other dark.

★157

there was thunder and lightning. A glimpse of the sea, crests of waves, and yes, there! dolphins, diving with the waves. A flash of the city, sugar blocks ahead. Through the clouds the city was getting closer, roaring closer. Passing so close to the city, would we graze the buildings? Seeing inside drawing rooms, flashes of people, washing on balconies, and then, once we had landed, and the plane wheeled around, Beirut entire, hovering on a heat haze. I thought I heard a chorus of people. In that first sight of Beirut I thought that I could hear the woven sound of many people singing, joined in pain and feeling. It didn't seem impossible to hear such a sound from this ancient city built on rock.

The joke was on me for packing an evening dress. This was not the Lebanon of Chelsea. The whole school met me, we sang to each other on the bus and when, wide-eyed, I first saw the mountains, I remember seeing the piles of rubbish and houses built on top of each other and thinking of the villages as ant heaps. Finally in the remote village of Deirkouche we were met by a delegation of villagers and sat in a little room, which I thought was the cloakroom. It turned out to be the room I would live in for the next two years with two other women and a child. But those were first impressions. Later I would look down from the schoolyard and see the village whole. See the women hanging washing on the roofs, an old man following his burdened donkey up a road, people greeting each other on their daily circuits. Below was a valley with a river running through an orange grove. Beyond was the Mediterranean where the sun set, fat and orange. Behind were snowcapped mountains and a monastery whose towers with golden tips caught the last of the sun. Most intoxicating of all were the blue nights

when the moon was so strong that you could see the shadows of the pine trees on the other side of the valley.

I was born again in Deirkouche. I don't mean that I found religion but that I learnt how to live again. Everything in front of me made sense, cohered and was strange. The villagers taught me how to smile, how to show teeth and let my smile reach my eyes. My first teachers were a family of women next to the school. Sheik Anisa was widowed with three daughters. They were poor but their white linen headscarves were blindingly white in the sunshine and their house was filled with mountain breezes. They taught me how to eat communally with bread instead of knives and forks, how to combine olive oil, lemons and garlic and make wonderful food. If they had something special for supper, they would save some for me, even when they hadn't eaten enough themselves. Later, a Beiruti friend was dismissive of Sheik Anisa's mountain speech and mountain ways, but I knew that she and her daughters were noble. They concentrated on making me happy and the slough of English loneliness left me. I became a daughter of Deirkouche. When I travelled back from a weekend in the city and saw the black and white traditional dress of the Druze, I knew I was protected.

That's not to say that it was an easy time. Hardly anyone spoke English and I was just starting to learn Arabic. It's incredibly difficult to keep tiny children together if you don't have the words for 'come back'. But I drew cartoons, sang, mimed, amused with yoga positions, did whatever I could to communicate, and the children were ready to play along. One day I was particularly discouraged, probably because of my ongoing and unsuccessful attempts to stop the

It's incredibly difficult to keep tiny children together
if you don't have the words for 'come back'.

headmistress hitting the children with a stick. In a free period I slipped away, climbed up the mountain and sat on a rock and thought about giving up. And then I tuned into the children singing below. Within laughter and screams, I could hear an accented chanting of 'Oranges and Lemons'. So, miraculously, something was being communicated. I climbed down from my rock and joined in the game: 'Atishoo, Atishoo, we all fall down'.

The village, which felt so safe and cohesive, was to fall under a shadow. One day, an Israeli F16 fighter plane flew over and the children scattered. One of the oldest and sweetest of the boys picked up a fallen branch ready to fire in protection of his friends, and I realized it would be the bravest who would die first.

Luckily these mountains were not involved in the fighting during the Israeli invasion of the summer of 1982. That was about to happen in West Beirut, beneath us, and it was to be heavier than any bombardment had ever been before.

At the beginning of that summer I heard Israeli Prime Minister Begin announce on the BBC World Service that Israel would not make the first move to start a war. At the same time I heard Israeli F16 fighter planes begin to bomb the coastal town of Damour. That weekend I had arranged to meet a friend at a taxi rank in Beirut. The bombing was heavy there and I feared I had sent him to his death. I decided to carry on in the taxi because he would be there looking for me. We edged forward into panicked streets. The taxi driver would go no further and so I walked. A villager turned militiaman saw me and directed me towards a safe house. And so I was caught up in West Beirut during the invasion of 1982.

There were opportunities to leave but I think I stayed because I wanted to witness and report back on an unequal war. Western media had prepared for this invasion. I had heard several talks and book reviews on the World Service with the same message. Israel was America's policeman or garbage collector in the Middle East. The Palestinians needed to be cleaned away, Lebanon needed cleaning. The same verbs were used in Arabic.

Eventually I enrolled as a volunteer at the American University Hospital (one certain way of getting food). I worked as an untrained nurse assisting the doctors, checking vital signs, changing bandages, daily painting the terrible burns caused by phosphorus bombs. The oldest Palestinian fighter on the ward was 22. His eyes would lock into mine when the electricity failed because his breathing depended on my regular depression of his respiratory bag.

The worst day of the war began in the early hours of one morning. I was watching the breeze lift the curtain of my bedroom. I had been given a room in a student residence near the hospital and was lying awake marveling that despite the daily bombardment I was still alive, still had ten fingers. Then the echoing sounds of shelling began. People ran into the corridors and I was urged to join them on their way to some cellar in a science building. I didn't want that. There were bombs that sought heat and homed in on bodies in bunkers. I didn't want to sit waiting for that. I thought about who I wanted to die with and made a run for the hospital and the ward I worked on.

We were being shelled from the sea, the air, the mountains and East Beirut. The ER stank of blood but also of work, of all of us working together to save lives. I greeted my co-workers: Bassam, gentle, generous and not old enough to have outgrown his acne; Valeria, a Filipino nurse bewildered by this war. We were glad to see each other briefly before we attended to the patients. Walking the corridors was like walking a tightrope. They seemed narrow and the glass on the other side revealed exploding hell. The patients attended to us. They had already seen this hell from the inside and had survived. Eyes reassured eyes, we kept each other going. Our actions were reassuringly uncomplicated: there was no doubt about the need to change a bandage, clean a chest

enrolled for a Masters in English Literature at the American University of Beirut and taught composition. I went back to Britain briefly but felt out of place. No one would understand why I cowered when planes passed. I was too caught up in the Lebanese story to leave yet. Teaching was easy, because the students, who came from warring militias, were eager to get on with their lives. They competed with each other to make jokes in English and taught themselves.

These images and stories seem far away from that Kentish lane of my childhood. Edward Said once told me that I should write about

## In order to live together, talk to each other, we need to learn where each of us comes from and how we got here. We need to go back...

tube, paint sterilizing cream onto burns. Our minds were clear and focused. At some point in the night I needed sleep and took the elevator to a random floor in search of somewhere quiet.

The elevator opened to a place of humming blue light. I had no idea where I was. I felt I had somehow slipped out of time. And then I saw incubators and figures standing by them. It was the obstetrics ward. Babies had just been born and had been wheeled into the centre of the building and were being guarded by tired mothers and family. Outside buildings were exploding and here babies were being born. I found somewhere to sleep and slept profoundly.

After the Israeli invasion of the summer of 1982, which began in South Lebanon and eventually succeeded in driving out Arafat's army from its retreat to West Beirut, I

my years in Deirkouche, because if I didn't that experience would be lost. When I talk about the invasion, those memories roll out at length. But the experience of war taught me the value of the village.

The village is why Lebanon was never anarchic. There were massacres and revenge killings, but never at random. Fellow villagers immediately support each other. Even in New York these village ties hold and a senator will help an electric goods salesman, simply because they are both sons of the same village. In order to live together, talk to each other, we need to learn where each of us comes from and how we got here. We need to go back metaphorically at least to the village, so as to trace the paths that brought us to this moment.

# TABLEAU: A SISTERHOOD IN SILENCE

MARY RORICH

Michele, hand on thigh, leaned into thought
and computer, leaving genetic structures for a
while to journey into territories of the past.

Moyra, blonde head bowed into the truths
of how communities think and believe, her
anchored stillness inviolate now.

Norma, framed against gentle tree breezes,
anorak thrown off in the passion of
remembering boys' initiations and hard black
journeys.

Margaret, loose-knitted jersey mirroring deep-
blue eyes, slender neck tattooed for courage,
caring (too much?) for truth and for her sisters;
reminding them gently of their worth.

Claudia, mother of beautiful, raped children,
explores the rich vocabularies of a self
nurtured in the wisdom and memory of
women who sense and see and write.

Tracy stalks by in long purple artist's cloak,
her iron curls uncompromising in integrity;
her beetles and flowers vivid as her inner life.

Sigrid wears her vulnerable, sensitive
interiority behind her 'Sting' T-shirt, thinks
of Vienna in the winter and sad Romania,
her beloved patterns imprinted in a smile of
the mind's eye.

Pam in dark blue velvet, a wide-eyed gazelle
of gentleness and chiselled bones, a teacher,

lover, generous in time and praise, framing her own bold oriental adventures with a calm soul.

Brenda, tortoise-shell clips holding back a girl's shining hair, lets the words tumble through, of joy, of dreams and of hopes; of pain, too, for women in a man's world, and outsiders and doing it alone, for love.

Susan's dark hair bobs above a rhythm of sad humour, engaging surrealist anamorphic images and stories of students who suck pipettes of sulphuric acid and do not die (quite).

Mary lives beyond the usual split of head and heart in this moment at De Hoek, drowning in words and confidentiality and danger.

There's bold Leah outside, braving the slight chill in beads; framing our contexts and creativities within patriarchal structures; thinking sensuously, also, about a sociology of chocolate.

Jane didn't marry a farmer at sixteen. She carries her wit as a shell for inner turmoil, her passionate understanding, sangoma-like, questioning what we say and how we say it. Flying above institutional drudgery like an angel in Chagall.

These women writing their lives, all flying like angels in Chagall. Flying, falling, then getting up to fly again.

# EPILOGUE - THE WONDERWOMAN PROJECT

MARGARET ORR

## THE PROBLEM

In 2002, the WonderWoman project began as brainchild of collaborative work between Professor Margaret Orr, Director of the Centre for Learning, Teaching, & Development, and Dr Wendy Orr, Director of Transformation & Employment Equity, at the University of the Witwatersrand. The trigger was the equity office's observation that the gender demographics for academic staff at Wits (in common with those at most other universities[1]) were cause for concern. In 2001, women represented 42.7% of senior lecturers, but only 19.4% of associate professors and 16.9% of full professors. There were no female Deans, and only one woman member of the senior executive team. The graph was depressing:

When we asked Deans, heads of schools and other senior academic staff to explain this trend, the lack of a sufficiently robust research and publication record was the most commonly cited reason for the failure of women to advance through the academic ranks. We thus originally conceived of the WonderWoman project as a type of 'publish, don't perish' programme, with a concentrated focus on writing retreats and writers' groups as impetus towards moving the bulge on the graph upwards.

We had barely begun work, however, when it became clear that the solution was not quite that simple. A host of interconnected structural, social, cultural and psychological factors are woven together in a pattern of disadvantage that many women find hard to overcome.

## POTHOLES IN THE PLAYING FIELD

The most cursory of research[2] revealed some potholes in the supposedly level playing fields. For example, in a test using the real-life CV of a (female) psychologist, researchers produced two copies of the CV, one with a fictional female name, and one with a fictional male name. They sent one of the versions out to 238 heads of schools and asked whether they thought the candidate was suitable for hiring. The participants

---

1. At Harvard in 2005, women held only 19% of tenured positions within the Humanities, and just 8% in the Sciences.
2. Collings, Lynn H., Joan C. Chrisler, Kathryn Quina (eds). 1998. *Career Strategies for Women in Academe: Arming Athena*. Sage Publications. Thousand Oaks, California.
   Fidell, L. S. 1975. 'Empirical Verification of Sex Discrimination in Hiring Practices in Psychology,' in R. K. Unger and F. L. Denmark, (eds.), Women: Dependent or Independent Variable? *Psychological Dimensions*, New York .
   Paludi, M.A. and L. A. Strayer. 1985. 'What's in an Author's Name? Different Evaluations of Performance as a Function of Author's Name,' *Sex Roles: A Journal of Research*, 12 (1985) pp. 353–361.
   Paludi, M. A. and W. D. Bauer. 1983. 'Goldberg Revisited: What's in an Author's Name,' *Sex Roles: A Journal of Research*, 9 (1983) pp. 387–390.
   Steinpreis, R.E., Anders, K. A., & Ritzke, D. 1999. 'The impact of gender on the review of the curricula vitae of job applicants and tenure candidates: A National Empirical Study.' *Sex Roles: A Journal of Research*, Vol 41, Nos 7/8, pp 509-528
   (Footnote 2 continued on next page)

were significantly more likely to recommend the hiring of the 'male' candidate. Similar results were obtained in a test using research articles submitted to editors of refereed journals. Research also seems to indicate that student evaluations of lecturers tend to be significantly more critical of female than of male lecturers[3]. Women academics tend to carry a disproportionate share of first year teaching, administration and committee work, and pastoral care and counseling of students – none of which carry significant weight in impressing selection committees. And then there are the ubiquitous second-shift domestic responsibilities which are also typically part of a female academic's workload. It became clear that we would have to do a far more comprehensive empowerment exercise than merely a number of writing workshops.

## THE SUCCESS STORIES

In November 2001, we held focus groups with senior women academics in an attempt to determine what critical factors had helped them 'make it' to the upper rungs of the academic career ladder. Two groups of senior women (academics at the level of professor, associate professor and head of school) were asked to explore with us the hurdles, hindrances, and hiccups; the challenges, the changes and the childbearing that had characterized the trajectories of their academic careers.

We asked them the following kinds of questions:

- Did you plan at the outset of your career to become a professor?
- When did you realize that you were good at your job? What was the catalyst?
- Did you plan marriage childbearing etc to accommodate your career trajectory?
- What are the critical factors affecting your ability to do your job well? (External?/Internal?)
- Do you feel successful? Does the environment of the university respond to you as if you were successful?
- What have you sacrificed in order to have an academic career?
- What advice do you wish you had had as a young female academic?

Few participants had systematically planned their career. Most had become involved in academic work primarily because they loved their subject, and many because they were passionate about teaching. Many had found their career had progressed by fits and starts as they took time out to focus on children, or that it took a number of years for them to realize that they could 'make it' or 'go for it' in terms of academic promotion. In many cases, it was mentorship, inspiration or direction from a research supervisor, a head of department or senior colleague that spurred them into focused action. Patronage from and a collegial relationship with

(Footnote 2 continued)

Top, Titia J. 1991. 'Sex Bias in the Evaluation of Performance in the Scientific, Artistic, and Literary Professions: A Review'. *Sex Roles: A Journal of Research*, 24 (1991), pp. 73–106.

Wenners, C. and A. Wold. 1997. 'Nepotism and Sexism in Peer-Review', *Nature*, 387 (22 May 1997), pp. 341–343.

Wertheim, Margaret. 1997. *Pythagoras' Trousers: God, Physics and the Gender Wars*. W.W. Norton & Company.

Website: Is there bias for or against women in academia? http://homepages.inf.ed.ac.uk/perdita/GenderBias/

3. University of Washington Center for Institutional Change: Resources Website
   http://www.engr.washington.edu/advance/resources/

someone in a senior position was seen to be particularly advantageous.

There was general agreement that single-mindedness, ambition, commitment, and discipline were essential. Young female academics were urged to plan their careers and to commit themselves to research, at the cost of teaching, service, and administration if necessary. Women, we were told, have to become selfish, learn to say no, 'to own their ambition', and 'become more like men' in their pursuit of promotion. Competitiveness was seen as a particular feature of the university culture, creating a harsh environment where individuals are forced to look after their own interests, and succeed only if they put themselves first. The concern that women 'should pay their dues' and not become a case for special pleading was strongly voiced by some participants. There was a clear degree of consensus that being a token equity appointment does not make one feel successful, and that the most powerful antidote to sexism is excellence.

The group saw focus, determination and dedication as essential components of a scholarly career which, all admitted, has to be one of the most difficult careers to follow in terms of the juggling act and levels of excellence expected. Significant personal sacrifices and a re-prioritization of family interests were seen to be an inevitable cost of academic accomplishment. The path was called a 'hideous head-down and don't look up marathon' by one speaker, and other voices acknowledged that there is a 'terrible price' to pay for being a successful female academic.

## SMART WOMEN, FOOLISH CHOICES
The senior women academics emphasized that choices have consequences, and that young women need to be aware of these. Some 'bad' or unwise choices, in terms of career advancement, include:

- Being willing to accept a major-time or part-time appointment
- Taking time off to have or rear children
- Making frequent demands on your Head of School for time off for sick children or family emergencies
- Limiting your availability for extended late meetings, lunchtime meetings (because of school lifts), evening functions or overtime work
- Unwillingness to travel away from home to conferences
- Investing too much energy in teaching
- Agreeing to administrative 'dogsbody' work
- Taking on a secondment to some restructuring or other bureaucratic university project
- Expending time and effort on community service
- Researching 'soft' subjects, and publishing in local journals or non-accredited journals
- Involvement in the 'unglamourous' work – particularly foundation, support or bridging programmes
- Being modest or retiring about your achievements

## THE OLD BOYS' CLUB
Some voices in the group skewered the subtle and insidious bias towards male culture at the university, and acknowledged the serious impediments this poses to women. Mention was made of the 'clubbiness of the Senate Room' and the intimidating atmosphere created for the few female members of Senate; the Head of School who starts looking bored and distracted as soon as a female professor begins to speak; the chairman of committees

★167

# LYNDA CARTER PAPER DOLL

1942 COSTUME
YEOMAN DIANA PRINCE
AMAZON PRINCESS DIANA

who calls men by their titles and women by their first names; the selection committees that are entirely male; the unease of being the only female member of a committee or department; the positioning of women as 'strident' or 'bossy' when they are assertive; the intolerance and contempt for the demands faced by women bearing the brunt of parenting; the expectation that women will pour the tea or take the notes in meetings; the inconsistent and seemingly arbitrary standards and criteria applied to promotions or performance appraisal of men and women; the fossilized attitudes and resistance in some members of the male establishment; the need for women to work twice as hard to earn equal recognition. There was recognition for the fact that a great deal of the core business work of the institution is carried by women, but that much of it is invisible and unrecognized.

As the afternoons wore on, a number of participants admitted to the Imposter or Cinderella Syndrome – that they really had got where they were through 'faking it' or 'busking' and that sooner or later their true inadequacies would be exposed. There was a rueful admission that the university culture is a hard and unsupportive one – affirmation and recognition are rare, while envy, spite and criticism are all too common an experience for all academics, regardless of gender. There was consensus that a more supportive environment was desirable, that mentorship should be more widely instituted, that goalposts and options in the academic career trajectory need to be made clearer and more explicit, that Heads of Schools need to ensure that workload is fairly and appropriately distributed, and that there needs – ideally – to be recognition of the widest possible range of contributions to the university's life and work.

## THE 'STRUGGLE' STORIES

We followed our meetings with supposedly 'successful' senior women academics with a focus group for the aspirant wannabes (all at the level of lecturer or senior lecturer) – the fifteen volunteer participants in our first planned WonderWoman programme. We asked for their perceptions of the hindrances and stumbling blocks in their way and were given a perspective somewhat different from that of the senior academics, a number of whom had claimed never to have experienced any discrimination at all.

A key problem identified was the absence of support, direction, and mentorship. Goalposts are unclear, and criteria for promotion and performance success are unspecified and seem to be whimsically applied. Conflicting messages are sent out: women are overloaded and exploited in terms of being 'dumped' with the unpopular courses, the dogsbody work, the drudgery of committees, the responsibility for re-designing curricula, academic support, or overhauling unworkable courses, but when it comes to promotion or performance assessment, such work is dismissed as irrelevant or unimportant. Black women feel treated in an especially dismissive way, and non-South African women feel an additional handicap.

Male academics, we were told, tend to be treated as 'precious princes' and are generally not expected to take on anything like the administrative loads carried by women. We were told of the double standards that make networking and informal collegiality difficult to sustain.

The golf-course, drinks, dinner model that applies to the 'old boys club' is difficult to emulate for women. Different standards of informality apply to women, and drinking and inviting a male colleague to dinner are potentially risky endeavours for a female academic's reputation.

Members of the group expressed the concern that women who have succeeded are often particularly unsupportive of women in junior positions, and there is a perception that in the process of succeeding in a male environment they have had to deny their essential humanity, and have become 'bitter, driven, unhappy, ungenerous, and unwilling to mentor younger women'. There was a sense of an absence of good role models – women whom we would aspire to be like. Support from men, on the other hand, often comes across as grandfatherly and patronizing, and can ultimately have a disempowering effect.

Family responsibilities, particularly childcare, were mentioned as significant challenges by many of the participants. Some felt forced to make untenable choices in the years when children are dependent. For these women, time and the capacity to concentrate on academic work will only be liberated when their children are grown and gone. In addition, unsupportive spouses can make it very difficult for women to perform to full capacity in a professional environment. It was felt that the institution unrealistically expects academic women to come to them without a background or baggage, and to become one-dimensional, forgetting that they are mothers, daughters, friends, and wives.

Lack of self esteem, low confidence in one's own abilities, and the inability to unselfconsciously showcase one's abilities were another common theme. Women in traditionally male faculties or schools felt particularly vulnerable about their position as 'politically correct appointees'.

Research output was identified as a stumbling block, with many participants feeling a lack of direction or focus in what to research and where to publish. Many felt insecure and in need of a reader whom they could trust to engage usefully with their argument and approach, rather than just comment on superficial issues. There was also a fairly bewildering sense of shifting goalposts – not all research seems to be equally valued, but the rules and criteria are not always clear. Merely 'counting publications' does not always provide a fair assessment of an individual's scholarly worth (it was noted that Isaac Newton had published only one paper in his entire lifetime, which would have qualified him to be a Junior Lecturer at Wits). On the other hand, some kinds of research or scholarly output seem not to count at all.

In discussing our plans for the WonderWoman Programme we debated useful interventions both in empowering and enabling the women themselves, and in challenging the academy to reflect on its own practices and discourse. The equation goes like this: If the Academy is A, and we add women and black people, does A+B still have to equal A? Or should the academy interrogate its tacit and hidden practices, and undergo true transformation to arrive at A+B=C? There was a strong sense that 'the rules of the game' need to be clarified, and in some cases challenged if the academy is to be truly transformed and not remain an institution that continues to be populated by white men – some of them in dresses and some of them with black skins, but all of them playing the same game.

## THE SOLUTION?

At the time of writing, four cohorts of WonderWomen have been through the programme, and since 2004, two cohorts have been through a similar programme, called GlassBusters, aimed at black academic staff (both men and women). Although the programme has been modified over the years, and is always individually customized to the needs of the particular cohort, a strong and consistent core has been extended writing retreats. Other interventions – less obviously utilitarian or goal directed – have included negotiation skills, voice and presentation skills, leadership skills, conflict resolution, assertiveness, time and stress management, values and work-life balance, executive coaching, diversity training, image workshops, workplace resilience, impact self defence, and spanner & wench. The latter two workshops have participants kicking the hell out of padded male instructors and changing a tyre, respectively, and have tended to have far more noticeable effects on women's assertiveness in meetings, their ability to patrol their own personal boundaries, and the capacity to say 'No' to doing work that they don't want to do and that will not advance their careers, than have the more traditional assertiveness workshops[4].

The successes of this programme are hard to pin down in quantifiable terms. The overall research output of the participants has tended to increase, and there have been a number of promotions[5]. Many of the elected lecturer representatives on Senate are now graduate WonderWomen, and most of them included this fact in their introductory CV presented to Senate. Senior male staff at the university have become twitchy, and after an initial period of fondly indulgent smiles, moved through a brief period of wittily referring to the 'WonderBra Project', and from there to a gravely expressed concern that we have created unsettling cabals of women who network and caucus and share ideas ahead of meetings, vote as a block in meetings, assert their rights to higher salaries, and generally make their male colleagues feel like insecure outsiders. Some heads have complimented the programme on creating a noticeable transformation and blossoming in female members of staff. Many participants have said that the programme has changed their lives, and has made a significant difference in how they felt about themselves, and about Wits. There have been some spectacular failures, and no single intervention can achieve everybody's individual transformation and empowerment goals, let alone those of an entire institution. The endeavour continues, and with each cohort, we learn new ways to improve the intervention.

---

4. When Linda Babcock asked why so many male graduate students were teaching their own courses and most female students were assigned as assistants, her Dean said: 'More men ask. The women just don't ask.' It turns out that whether they want higher salaries or more help at home, women often find it hard to ask. Sometimes they don't know that change is possible--they don't know that they can ask. Sometimes they fear that asking may damage a relationship. And sometimes they don't ask because they've learned that society can react badly to women asserting their own needs and desires. *Women Don't Ask: Negotiation and the Gender Divide* Linda Babcock and Sara Laschever Princeton University Press 2003 http://www.pupress.princeton.edu/chapters/i7575.html

5. Overall demographics for Wits are obviously not attributable directly to our empowerment programmes, but do show an upward trend. In 2005 women constitute 44.4% of senior lecturers, 25.4% of associate professors, and 22.2% of professors (in comparison to the 2001 figures of 42.7%, 19.4% and 16.9 %). Unfortunately, at the time of writing, we still had no female Deans, and only one woman on the senior executive team.

# CONTRIBUTORS

**PROFESSOR JANE CASTLE** Born in Scotland, raised in Canada, and ripened in Germany, Jane has lived in South Africa for 25 years. Nurturing an ambition to be a writer and farmer, she completed a BA in English in Canada. She was diverted into the field of adult education in Germany, where she taught English to businessmen and Turkish guest workers. Jane came to Wits in the 1980s as a mature student and completed her M.Ed and PhD while working as a lecturer. She became an Associate Professor on 1 April 2003. The WonderWoman programme has helped Jane to 'come out' as a writer, and she is presently composing her first book.

**DR SUSAN CHEMALY** was born in Johannesburg and has lived there all her life, except for a brief excursion to Pittsburgh USA (sixteen months) and a much longer one to Pretoria, where she lectured in Inorganic Chemistry at UNISA for sixteen years. All her degrees (BSc, BScHons and PhD) were obtained at Wits University. She has lectured in three departments at Wits, Chemistry, Biochemistry, and Pharmacy and Pharmacology, where she is presently Senior Lecturer in Pharmaceutical Chemistry. Her favourite molecule and the subject of her research is vitamin B12; she has published nineteen articles in academic journals. Her hobbies and interests are reading, aerobics, walking, photography, and birdwatching.

**PROFESSOR LEAH GILBERT** holds undergraduate degrees from the Hebrew University, Jerusalem and a PhD from Wits. Employed at Wits since 1978, she has been involved in teaching social and behavioural sciences in a variety of health disciplines. This provided the background for a widely used reader: *Society, Health and Disease*. Her research interests are reflected in her publications on topics such as social aspects of Dentistry, Pharmacy in Primary Health Care, Globalisation and Health, Medical Pluralism, Social Inequalities and HIV/AIDS. Her current research focuses on the impact of HIV/AIDS on the various health professions, as well as the social complexities of adherence to Anti-Retroviral Therapy.

**DR SIGRID EWERT** joined Wits in September 2000 as Lecturer in Computer Science, and was promoted to Senior Lecturer in April 2003. She was awarded her doctorate in February 1999 by the University of Stellenbosch for a thesis in formal language theory, and subsequently spent a year as postdoctoral fellow in Germany. Since 1996 she has maintained a steady publication output, and consequently was rated an established researcher by the National Research Foundation in 2001. She has obtained several scholarships and grants, the most recent being a substantial grant for joint research with Swedish and local scientists. She teaches undergraduate and Honours students, and has extensive experience in university administration.

**DR MOYRA KEANE** – HED (Physics; Chemistry, Natal), BA (Psychology, UNISA), MSc (Wits), PhD (Wits) – works as an Academic Development Advisor in the Teaching and Learning Centre in the Faculty of Science. This involves lecturing, working on policy, strategy, curriculum, staff development and research. Moyra has worked in curriculum materials development, outreach programmes, management, consultancy and education for 22 years. Her interests include multicultural education and participative research. Walking around Mt Kailas in Tibet, rafting on the Zambezi, trekking to the gorillas in Uganda and leading of wilderness trails have been some of the adventures that have stretched and sustained her.

**ALISON KEARNEY** completed a Masters Degree in Fine Arts at Wits University in February 2005. She has received a number of awards, including the Standard Bank History of Art Award and The Johannesburg Art Gallery History of Art Award (2002). In 2003 she was a finalist for the MTN New Contemporaries Art Award, and 2004 she was artist in residence at The IAAB artists studio's in Basel Switzerland. In 2005 she was artist in residence at The Gertrude Contemporary Art Space in Australia, making art for *The Next Wave Festival* that took place in Melbourne in March 2006. Alison works part time as a Design Theory lecturer at Johannesburg University and as a Theory and Practice lecturer in the Art Department of the Wits School of Education. She has participated in a number of group exhibitions in South Africa and abroad and held her first solo exhibition at The Johannesburg Art Gallery in February 2005.

**BRENDA KEEN** decided to become an accountant at the age of twelve. She obtained a BComm and BAcc from Wits, completed articles with KPMG and qualified as a chartered accountant in 1990. In 1995 she completed a BA through Unisa, with a distinction in Psychology. She joined the support staff of Wits University in 2001. Initially the Payroll Office reported to her and she worked on the Annual Financial Statements. She is currently responsible for Fees & Debtors and the Creditors Office. Brenda has a son and daughter, and intends to keep on writing in her spare time. She plans to move to the edge of reality and commute.

PROFESSOR TRACY MCLELLAN was educated at the Massachusetts Institute of Technology and the Woods Hole Oceanographic Institution. She has worked at eight different universities, including, most recently and for the longest period of time, Wits, where she is currently Associate Professor of Molecular and Cell Biology. Her research has taken her to the deep sea in a submersible, to the forests of Trinidad and South Africa and the sand dunes of the California coast, and to AIDS clinics. She has published articles in scientific journals and popular magazines on evolution and genetics in plants, people and fishes. Her long term goal is to make patchwork quilts with tartans and batiks.

DR PAMELA NICHOLS was born in the UK and holds degrees in English and in Comparative Literature from the universities of Sussex and New York. She has taught ESL, expository writing and comparative literature in Lebanon, Jordan, New York and Johannesburg. She was drawn to South Africa after hearing Helen Suzman comment that South Africa has the legislation but not yet the culture of a democracy. She is Director of the Wits Writing Centre where she is responsible for writing consultation services and writing workshops for students and academic staff. She is currently writing about the work of the Writing Centre and putting together a photo-essay of Lebanon in collaboration with award-winning photographer Debbie Yazbek.

PROFESSOR MARGARET ORR is Director of the Centre for Learning, Teaching, & Development at the University of the Witwatersrand. She holds degrees in English from the University of Pretoria, the University of South Africa, and the University of Washington (as a Fulbright scholar). She is the author or co-author of seven textbooks in the field of English language skills and usage, of a number of articles covering an eclectic range of academic interests (including gender issues, academic leadership, online learning, creativity, and performance management), and of a multitude of tedious university policy documents.

DR WENDY ORR qualified as a medical doctor at UCT in 1983. She served in the District Surgeon's Office in Port Elizabeth in 1985 and was responsible for a famous Supreme Court interdict which revealed for the first time that police were systematically torturing and abusing political detainees. She has practised as a doctor in the NGO, public and private sectors and served as a commissioner on South Africa's Truth and Reconciliation Commission. From 1999 to 2005 she was the Director of Transformation & Employment Equity at the University of the Witwatersrand, and in that role was responsible for co-development with Margaret Orr of a number of donor-funded equity development initiatives. She is currently exploring life after Wits as a consultant.

PROFESSOR MARY RORICH is Associate Professor of Musicology in the Wits School of Arts. She studied at the Universities of Cape Town, Cambridge and Wits, and holds a PhD in her subject. She has published in her specialist areas of opera, 20th-century western art music, gender and South African music. Mary is also a public lecturer, music critic and broadcaster, and was the radio diva behind 'Classic Soaps', 'Swoon Tunes' and other programmes on South Africa's Classic FM. Mary has one daughter, an aging cat, a Steinway grand piano and great plans for travelling more and writing a number of books, including an autobiography.

DR NORMA M. NONGAUZA-TSOTSI was born in Langa location, Cape Town. She studied in Zimbabwe, Scotland, Romania and Johannesburg and has spent parts of her life in North America, South America, Italy and Lesotho where she was a nurse, student, housewife, and dentist. She was well over thirty years old when she completed her Masters degree in Public Health at Wits and her life as an academic has been relatively brief. She is currently chief dentist, lecturer, researcher and service provider in the School of Public Health at the University of the Witwatersrand, responsible for coordinating and teaching Public Health courses to undergraduate dental students.

ABOUT THE PHOTOGRAPHS BY ALISON KEARNEY The photographic essay in this volume is made up of a series of images that document walks around the Wits campus, and which focus specifically on the details of the journey which are generally overlooked: that which is beneath the surface. Some photographs combine images taken from Wits archives in a palimpsest of present and past. In focussing on what is usually not noticed, the essay emphasizes a particular quality of attention; a particular way of looking, and the photographs are presented as a visual journey of discovery for the reader.